Anonymous

Welcome Songs

Anonymous

Welcome Songs

ISBN/EAN: 9783337265663

Printed in Europe, USA, Canada, Australia, Japan

Cover: Foto ©Thomas Meinert / pixelio.de

More available books at **www.hansebooks.com**

No. 1. WOULD YOU HAVE YOUR LIFE ALL SUNSHINE

DAVID C. COOK.

T. MARTIN TOWNE.

1. Would you have your life all sun-shine, Do you want its wor-ries o'er?
   Yield your-self to Je-sus ful-ly, Trust His love [Omit. . . .]
2. It will bright-en all life's griev-ing, It will gild its cloud-ed sky;
   It will make its pains your glo-ry, Smil-ing, you [Omit.]

and want no more.
shall dare to die.

CHORUS.

Come, then, come in-to the full-ness Of the light of

Je-sus' love, Yield your life to His blest guidance, You shall dwell with Him a-bove.

3 Have you time to give to love Him,
  For communion by the way?
  Take Him, then, as your companion,
  Keep Him with you all the day.

4 Do you long for rest and heaven,
  He your rest and heaven shall be,
  Cast on Him your every burden,
  Rest in Him eternally.

No. 2.   MORE LIKE JESUS.

Rev. A. A. Hoskins.   Henry Tucker. By per

Moderato.

1. More like Je - sus, more like Je - sus, Ev - 'ry day   I long to be;
2. More like Je - sus, more like Je - sus, Safe with Him   my all shall be;
3. More like Je - sus, more like Je - sus, Ev - er - more   I hope to be,

Sav-ior, hear my soul's pe-ti - tion, Give my heart Thy glad fru - i - tion,
Oh, the glad-ness of a - bid - ing In the safe - ty of the hid - ing,
On-ward thro' this whole life go-ing, Then thro' heav'nly a - ges grow-ing,

CHORUS.

Make me more and more like Thee.)
Je-sus, living more like Thee. }
Je-sus, more and more like Thee.)

More and more,   more and more,

More and more,   more and more,

More and more like Je-sus ev-'ry day,   ev'ry day, More and more like Jesus.
ev-'ry day,

No. 3. EVER TRUE, EVER PURE.

MAGGIE W. SNODGRASS. T. MARTIN TOWNE. By per.

Allegretto.

1. Je - sus, make us   pure and spotless, White without and white within;
2. Far from us   be   all   de-cep - tion—Ev - 'ry word and   ac-tion mean;
3. Oh, the ten - der - ness and sor - row Blended in   a   Sav-ior's love;

Thou canst see be - neath the sur-face, Bring to light the   in - most sin.
Make the spir - it   right within   us, Touch the heart and make it clean.
Reach-ing thro' all   sin   to gath - er   To   the sheltered home a - bove.

CHORUS.

Ev-er true,...... ev-er   pure;.....This our watchword still shall be;
Ev-er true,   ever pure,   shall be;

Ev-er true,...... ev-er pure,..... E-ven, Je - sus, like to   Thee.
Ev-er true,   ev-er pure,

No. 4.　LOVE IS THE KEY.

KATE SUMNER BURR.　　　　　　　　T. MARTIN TOWNE. By per.

1. { On - ly the heart that is lov - ing can know,
   { On - ly the heart that is lov - ing can share
2. { On - ly the heart that is lov - ing can lie
   { On - ly the heart that is lov - ing can say
3. { On - ly the heart that is lov - ing can sing,
   { On - ly the heart that is lov - ing shall soar

CHORUS.

Free-dom from bond-age in serv-ice be-low; }
Sweet-est com-mun-ion with Je-sus in prayer. }
Calm-ly sub-mis-sive when sor-row is nigh; } Love is the key to
Je-sus is pre-cious by night and by day. }
Glo-ry to Je-sus. Re-deem-er and King; }
O - ver the riv-er to heaven's bright shore. }

bless-ings un-told. Love is the key, love is the key; Love is the

key to blessings un-told, Love is the beau-ti-ful key.

No. 5.   DARE TO DO RIGHT.

Rev. Geo. Lansing Taylor.   Wm. B. Bradbury.

1. Dare to do right! dare to be true! You have a work that no
2. Dare to do right! dare to be true! Je - sus, your Sav - ior, will

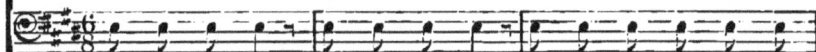

oth - er can do: Do it so brave-ly, so kind-ly, so well,
car - ry you thro'; Cit - y, and man-sion, and throne all in sight,

CHORUS.

An-gels will hast-en the sto-ry to tell. }
Can you not dare to be true and do right? } Dare, dare, dare to do right!

Dare, dare, dare to be true! Dare to be true! dare to be true!
Dare,

USED BY AN ARRANGEMENT WITH THE BIGLOW & MAIN CO.

No. 6. LIKE JESUS.

Arranged.

CHAS. EDW. POLLOCK.

Lively.

1. We'll try to be like Je - sus, The chil-dren's pre-cious Friend,
2. We'll try to be like Je - sus, In bod - y and in mind,
3. We'll try to be like Je - sus, And when we come to die.

Far dear - er than a moth - er, He loves us to the end.
For He was true and lov - ing, And to each per - son kind.
At His right hand in glo - ry, With an - gels live on high.

CHORUS.

We'll try, we'll try, We'll try to be like Je - sus,
We'll try to be like Je - sus,

Like Je - sus, like Je - sus, The chil-dren's dear - est Friend.

No. 7. OH, WON'T YOU BE A CHRISTIAN?

A. A. G.

1. Oh, won't you be a Chris-tian While you're young? Oh,
2. Oh, won't you love the Sav - ior While you're young? Oh,
3. Re - mem - ber, death may find you While you're young! Re-

won't you be a Chris - tian While you're young? Don't
won't you love the Sav - ior While you're young? For
mem - ber, death may find you While you're young: For

think it will be bet - ter To de - lay it un - til
you He left His glo - ry, And em - braced a cross so
friends are oft - en weep-ing, And the stars their watch are

lat - er, But re-mem-ber your Cre - a - tor While you're young?
go - ry: Won't you heed the melting sto - ry While you're young?
keeping O er the grass-y graves, where sleeping Lie the young.

4 ||:Oh, walk the path to glory
While you're young; :||
And Jesus will befriend you,
And from danger will defend you,
And a peace divine will send you
While you're young.

5 ||:Then won't you be a Christian
While you're young? :||
Why from the future borrow,
When, ere comes another morrow,
You may weep in endless sorrow
While you're young?

FROM "HAPPY VOICES," BY PERMISSION OF A. A. GRALEY.

Draw Me Close to Thee

D. C. C.

DAVID C. COOK.
Harmony, T. M. T.

No. 8.

1. Draw me close to Thee, Lord, Ev - er close to Thee·
2. Draw me close to Thee, Lord, Ev - er close to Thee:
3. Draw me close to Thee, Lord, Ev - er close to Thee:

Oth-er friends are fail-ing, Thou art all - a - vail-ing, Thou art all - pre-
Let me smile in sor - row, Care nor trouble bor - row, Fear not for the
Ev - 'ry need pro-vid - ing, In Thy love con-fid - ing, Clos - er still a-

CHORUS

vail - ing, Draw me close to Thee. }
mor - row, Ev - er close to Thee. } Clos - er, ev - er clos - er,
bid - ing Ev - er close to Thee. }

clos - er, Lord, to Thee. Clos-er, ev - er clos-er, clos-er, Lord, to Thee.

No. 9. 'TIS SO SWEET TO TRUST IN JESUS.

Mrs. Louisa M. R. Stead.   W. J. Kirkpatrick.

1. 'Tis so sweet to trust in Je - sus, Just to take Him at His word;
2. Yes, 'tis sweet to trust in Je - sus, Just from sin and self to cease;
3. I'm so glad I learned to trust Thee, Precious Je-sus, Sav-ior, Friend;

Just to rest up - on His promise; Just to know, "Thus saith the Lord."
Just from Je - sus sim-ply tak-ing Life, and rest, and joy and peace.
And I know that Thou art with me, Wilt be with me to the end.

REFRAIN.

Je - sus, Je - sus, how I trust Him: How I've prov'd Him o'er and o'er,

Je - sus, Je - sus, pre-cious Je - sus! Oh, for grace to trust Him more.

TRIM YOUR LAMP.

E. LENA GRISWOLD.　　　　　　　　　T. MARTIN TOWNE.

No. 10.

1. Now trim your lamp for Je-sus, Let not your light be dim;
2. Now trim your lamp for Je-sus, Nor let it hid-den be;
3. Now trim your lamp for Je-sus; 'Tis He who bids you shine;
4. Then trim your lamp for Je-sus, Nor deem it e'er a cross

Full well He knows each ac - tion That you may do for Him.
Be not a-shamed of Je - sus, He's not a - shamed of thee.
And His shall be the glo - ry, A crown of life be thine.
To brave - ly shine for Je - sus 'Mid earth-ly sin and loss.

CHORUS.

Then trim your lamp for Je - sus, And to your faith be true;

The world will judge of Je - sus By what they see in you.

No. 11. GATHER UP THE SUNBEAMS.

Mrs. Albert Smith.   T. Martin Towne.

1. Let us gath-er up the sun-beams Ly-ing all a-round our path:
2. Strange we nev-er prize the mu-sic Till the sweet-voiced bird is flown!
3. If we knew the ba-by fin-gers, Pressed against the window pane,
4. Ah! those lit-tle ice-cold fin-gers, How they point our mem'ries back

Let us keep the wheat and ros-es, Cast-ing out the thorns and chaff,
Strange that we should slight the violets Till the love-ly flow'rs are gone!
Would be cold and stiff to-mor-row— Nev-er troub-le us a-gain—
To the hast-y words and ac-tions Strewn a-long our backward track!

Let us find our sweetest com-fort In the bless-ings of to-day,
Strange that summer skies and sunshine Nev-er seem one half so fair,
Would the bright eyes of our dar-ling Catch the frown up-on our brow?—
How those lit-tle hands re-mind us, As in snow-y grace they lie,

D.S.—*Let us find our sweet-est com-fort In the bless-ings of to-day,*

D.S.

With a pa-tient hand re-mov-ing All the bri-ars from the way.
As when winter's snow-y pin-ions Shake the white down in the air!
Would the prints of ros-y fin-gers Vex us then as they do now?
Not to scat-ter thorns—but ros-es— For our reap-ing by and by.

With a pa-tient hand re-mov-ing All the bri-ars from the way.

No. 12. SPEAK KINDLY.

LUELLA CLARK.

L. E. JONES.

1. Speak kindly, speak kind-ly to young and to old; The words of true
2. Speak kindly, speak kind-ly; no tongue can ex-press The power of true
3. Speak kindly, speak kind-ly; kind words never yet Brought hatred or

kindness are better than gold; Kind words ev'ry morning, kind words ev'ry
kindness to cheer and to bless; It soothes ev'ry sorrow, makes smooth ev'ry
dis - cord or grief or re-gret; Speak kindly, speak kindly, and then never

night, And kind words for-ev - er, in dark days or bright. Kind words ev'ry
path; It light-ens all bur-dens and turns a-way wrath. It soothes ev'ry
fear; Life's li - lies and ros - es will bloom all the year. Speak kindly, speak

morning, kind words ev'ry night, And kind words forever, in dark days or bright.
sorrow, makes smooth ev'ry path; It lightens all burdens and turns away wrath.
kindly, and then nev-er fear; Life's lilies and roses will bloom all the year.

No. 13.

SAY NO!

O. D. Sherman.

C. E. Pollock. By per.

1. If on some pleas-ant Sab-bath day, A play-mate un-to
2. If Sa-tan ev-er pass-ing by, Should tempt to tell the
3. And so of ev-'ry path of sin, Your feet are prone to

you should say, From Sab-bath School let's stay a-way, And
smooth-est lie, De-ceive your par-ents on the sly, Don't
wan-der in, For if the crown of life you'd win, An

CHORUS.

spend the hour in fun and play,)
stop to ar-gue what or why; } Just say, No! A good, round, hearty
e-vil hab-it ne'er be-gin:)

No! By this, true manliness you'll show, And honor God by saying No!

JESUS FOR ME.

DAVID C. COOK.

T. MARTIN TOWNE.

No. 14.

1. On - ly by Him I walk, He is the way;
2. On - ly He knows the right; He is the truth;
3. On - ly by Him I live, He is my life;

In Him I can - not stray, No harm can reach the way,
In Him all truth I find, He gives each word that's kind,
He is my life and light, He prompts each act that's right,

CHORUS.

Leads to e - ter - nal day. He is the way.
He puts right tho'ts in mind, He is the truth. } Best of all friends is He,
He gives my hand its might, He is my life.

Lov - ing me con-stant-ly; Ev - er with Him to. be, Je - sus for me.

No. 15. ALWAYS SPEAK THE TRUTH.

J. W. PRATT.

1. Be the mat-ter what it may, Al-ways speak the truth:
2. There's a charm in ver-i-ty; Al-ways speak the truth;
3. False-hood sel-dom stands a-lone, Al-ways speak the truth;

Wheth-er work, or wheth-er play, Al-ways speak the truth.
But there's mean-ness in a lie, Al-ways speak the truth.
One be-gets an-oth-er one, Al-ways speak the truth.

Nev-er from this rule de-part; Grave it deep-ly on your heart;
He is but a cow-ard, slave, Who, a pres-ent pain to waive,
Falsehood all the soul degrades, Stains with sin and ev-er breeds

Writ-ten 'tis on vir-tue's chart, Al-ways speak the truth.
Stoops to false-hood; then be brave; Al-ways speak the truth.
E-vil thoughts and dark-er deeds; Al-ways speak the truth.

FROM "GOOD WILL," BY PERMISSION OF TOWNE & STILLMAN.

JESUS PILOT ME

No. 16.

J. E. GOULD.

FINE.

1. Je - sus, Sav - ior, pi - lot me O - ver life's tem-pest-uous sea;
D. C. *Chart and com-pass are from Thee; Je - sus, Sav - ior, pi - lot me.*

2. As a moth - er stills her child, Thou canst hush the o - cean wild;
D. C. *Wondrous Sovereign of the sea, Je - sus, Sav - ior, pi - lot me.*

3 When at last I near the shore, And the fear - ful break-ers roar,
D. C. *May I hear Thee say to me, "Fear not, I will pi - lot thee!"*

D. C.

Unknown waves be-fore me roll, Hid-ing rocks and treacherous shoal;
Boisterous waves o-bey Thy will When Thou say'st to them, "Be still! "
'Twixt me and the peaceful rest, Then, while lean-ing on Thy breast,

No. 17.   JESUS IS MINE.

1 Fade, fade each earthly joy,
    Jesus is mine!
Break every tender tie,
    Jesus is mine!
Dark is the wilderness,
Earth hath no resting place,
Jesus alone can bless,
    Jesus is mine.

2 Tempt not my soul away,
    Jesus is mine!

Here would I ever stay,
    Jesus is mine!
Perishing things of clay,
Born but for one brief day,
Pass from my heart away,
    Jesus is mine!

3 Farewell, mortality,
    Jesus is mine!
Welcome, eternity,
    Jesus is mine!
Welcome, O loved and blest,
Welcome, sweet scenes of rest,
Welcome, my Savior's breast,
    Jesus is mine.°

No. 18. NEVER MIND.

Rev. Henry Burton, M. A. T. Martin Towne.

Moderato.

1. Did you hear the an - gry word? Nev - er, nev - er mind;
2. Have you plann'd and toil'd in vain? Nev - er, nev - er mind;
3. Does the east wind rude - ly blow? Nev - er, nev - er mind;
4. Is the fu - ture all un-known? Nev - er, nev - er mind;

Let it be as nev - er heard; Nev - er, nev - er mind.
Loss sometimes is high - est gain, Nev - er, nev - er mind.
Does the north wind bring the snow? Nev - er, nev - er mind.
Thou wilt nev - er be a - lone, Nev - er, nev - er mind.

'Twill but rank-le in the breast, 'Twill but break thy spir-it's rest,
Hon - or is not bought and sold, Char-ac - ter is more than gold,
'Twould be south or 'twould be west. If thy Fa - ther tho't it best,
Turn a - bove thy weep-ing eyes, Heav'n is watch-ing thro' the skies,

Cast it from thee, that is best, Nev - er, nev - er mind.
These are yours, a wealth un - told, Nev - er, nev - er mind.
Face it like the vane, and rest, Nev - er, nev - er mind.
Trust the love that nev - er dies, Nev - er, nev - er mind.

No. 19.   I HAVE A FATHER.

L. H.

Lucius Hart.

1. I have a Father in the promised land, I have a Father
2. I have a Savior in the promised land, I have a Sav-ior
3. I have a crown in the promised land, I have a crown

in the prom-ised land, My Fa - ther calls me, I must go To
in the prom-ised land, My Sav - ior calls me, I must go To
in the prom-ised land, When Je - sus calls me, I must go To

Chorus.

meet Him in the prom-ised land. I'll a-way, I'll a-way to the
meet Him in the prom-ised land. I'll a-way, I'll a-way to the
wear it in the prom-ised land. I'll a-way, I'll a-way to the

prom-ised land, I'll a-way, I'll a - way to the prom-ised land,
prom-ised land, I'll a-way, I'll a - way to the prom-ised land,
prom-ised land, I'll a-way, I'll a - way to the prom-ised land,

I Have a Father.

My Father calls me, I must go   To meet Him in the promised land.
My Sav-ior calls me, I must go   To meet Him in the promised land.
When Je-sus calls me, I must go   To meet Him in the promised land.

No. 20. ## THE LORD WILL PROVIDE.

Mrs. M. A. W. Cook.   T. Martin Towne. By per.

1. In some way or oth-er the Lord will pro-vide; It may not be my way.
2. At some time or oth-er the Lord will pro-vide; It may not be my time,
3. Despond then no longer, the Lord will pro-vide; And this be the to-ken,

It may not be thy way, And yet in His own way, The Lord will provide.
It may not be thy time, And yet in His own time, The Lord will provide.
No word He hath spoken Was ev-er yet bro-ken; The Lord will provide.

CHORUS.

Then we'll trust in the Lord, Trust in the Lord, Then we'll trust in the Lord, And He will provide.

LOVE DIVINE.

F. H. CONVERSE.   W. F. SHERWIN. By per.

No. 21.

1 Oh, love divine and wondrous deep, How strong that Shepherd's claim,
2. I sought His blessed face a - lone, Bowed down with sin and shame;
3. Now gently guiding safe along, His care remains the same,

Who not alone doth lead His sheep, But call-eth each by name; His
He met me there in lov-ing tone, He called to me by name; And
Whose love ap-pear-eth ten-fold strong, Who knows His own by name; And

voice we hear and follow all, (fol-low all,) His guid-ing steps and gracious
wea - ry with my fruitless quest, (fruitless quest,) I told Him all and thus found
leads from out the shadows gray, (shadows gray,) His ransom'd up to per-fect

call, (gracious call,) Whose voice we hear and follow all, (follow all,) His guiding steps and gracious call.
rest, (thus found rest,) And weary with my fruitless quest, (fruitless quest,) I told Him all and thus found rest.
day, (perfect day,) And leads from out the shadows gray, (shadows gray,) His ransom'd up to perfect day.

No. 22. WHY BE ASHAMED TO OWN THE KING?

F. E. B.

F. E. BELDEN.

1. Never be ashamed to own your Sav-ior, He who owns and cares for you;
2. Never be ashamed to read your Bi - ble, Guide-book for the pil-grim way,
3. Never be ashamed to kneel, like Daniel, Asking help three times each day:
4. Never be ashamed to say "God loves me," And "I know that I'm forgiv'n;"

D. C. *Never be ashamed to own your Sav-ior, He who owns and cares for you;*

Never be ashamed to tell His goodness, He's a friend for-ev - er true.
Leading to a home of joy e - ter - nal, If its precepts we o - bey.
Fearing not the den or fier - y furnace, Trust in God, and watch and pray.
Hating ev'ry sin, and trust-ing Je - sus, We are heirs of God and heav'n.

Never be ashamed to tell His goodness, He's a friend for-ev - er true.

CHORUS.

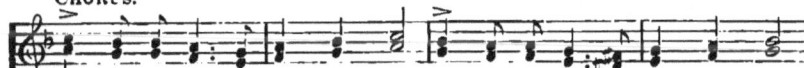

Why be ashamed to own the King? Why be ashamed His praise to sing?
Never be ashamed,   Never be ashamed,

D.C.

Why be ashamed your heart to bring? Why be a - shamed?
Nev-er be ashamed, no nev-er be ashamed of Him.

GOOD BYE

No. 23.

D. C. C.

DAVID C. COOK.

Harmony, T. M. T.

1. We are part-ing, we are part-ing; We are leav-ing one an-oth-er,
2. Je - sus bless you, Je-sus bless you; May His arms of love embrace you,
3. Je - sus keep you, Je - sus keep you, Day by day be watching o'er you,

And our voice in sweet-est cho-rus Wish you all a true good-bye.
With His sweetest words ca - ress you, May His bless-ings nev - er cease.
With His presence go be-fore you, From all dan - ger ev - er keep.

CHORUS.

So now we say good - bye,...... We bid you all good-bye,......
good-bye, good-bye,

May Je - sus keep you all the time, Good-bye to you, good-bye;....
good-bye.

No. 24.   BE GENTLE.

Arranged.   C. H. FYKE.

1. Ev - er let us each be   lov-ing, Show af - fec-tion, kind and true,
2. Ev - er let us each be   lov-ing, Nev - er give an - oth - er pain,
3. Be not sel-fish tow'rd each oth-er, Nev - er spoil an - oth-er's play;
4. Oh, be gen - tle, oh, be gen - tle, Oh, be gen - tle all the way,

Do - ing al-ways un - to oth - ers As to us we'd have them do.
If   a broth-er speak in an - ger, An-swer not in wrath a - gain.
Let us not of-fend in ac-tions, Nor in an - y-thing we say.
Thinking kind-ly, speaking kind - ly, Act - ing kind - ly ev - 'ry day.

CHORUS

Oh, be gen - tle with each oth - er; Oh, be care-ful day by day,

Let us not of - fend in ac-tions, Or by an - y-thing we say.

No. 25. WHAT MUST IT BE TO BE THERE!

Mrs. Elizabeth Mills.

Melody by J. H. Saylor.
Harmony by W. M. Beery.

1. We speak of the realms of the blest, That country so bright and so fair;
2. We speak of its pathways of gold, Its walls decked with jewels so rare,
3. We speak of its serv-ice of love, The robes which the glo-ri-fied wear,
4. O Lord, amidst gladness or woe, For heav-en our spir-its pre-pare:

And oft are its glo-ries confessed, But what must it be to be there!
Its wonders and pleasures untold; But what must it be to be there!
The church of the first-born above; But what must it be to be there!
And shortly we al-so shall know And feel what it is to be there.

Chorus.

To be there, to be there, ... Oh, what must it
To be there, to be there,

be to be there; With Je - sus our Friend, All e -
to be there,

What Must it Be to Be There!

Rit.

ter - ni - ty to spend, Oh, what must it be to be there!
to be there!

No. 26. HE CARES FOR YOU.

FANNY J. KENNISH.   T. MARTIN TOWNE.

1. He will watch o'er, He will guard you In sor-row and dan-ger, All His
2. On - ly seek ye for the kingdom; The rest shall be giv - en To His

CHORUS

loved ones, all His faith-ful Who trust in His name.
loved ones and His faith-ful Who trust in His name. } Take no tho't for the

morrow, Fear not pain nor sorrow; Seek not trouble to borrow, He careth for you.

I am His

DAVID C. COOK.　　　　　T. MARTIN TOWNE.

No. 27.

1. I am His, I am His, I'm not my own;
2. I am His, I am His, Won by His love;
3. I am His, I am His, Kept by His pow'r;
4. I am His, I am His, Al-ways to be:

All that I have and am is His, Is His a-lone.
Dear-est and best of earth is He, High-est a-bove.
Round me His lov-ing, might-y arms, Safe ev-'ry hour.
He gilds each day its pass-ing clouds, Heav'n waits for me.

CHORUS.

Al-ways with me, al-ways with me, Ev-'ry-where I go;

Al-ways with me, al-ways with me, All life's jour-ney through.

No. 28. GIVE ME JESUS.

FANNY J. CROSBY.   JNO. R. SWENEY.

1. Take the world, but give me Je-sus,— All its joys are but a name;
2. Take the world, but give me Je-sus, Sweet-est com - fort of my soul;
3. Take the world, but give me Je-sus, Let me view His con-stant smile;

But His love a - bid - eth ev - er, Thro' e - ter - nal years the same.
With my Sav - ior watching o'er me, I can sing, tho' bil-lows roll.
Then throughout my pilgrim jour-ney Light will cheer me all the while.

CHORUS.

Oh, the height and depth of mer - cy, Oh, the length and breadth of love,

Oh, the ful - ness of re-demp-tion, Pledge of end - less life a - bove.

WE ARE SOWING.

Mrs. E. A. Simes.

J. W. Slaughenhaup.
By per.

No. 29.

1. We are sowing, ev-er sowing, Worthless seed or golden
2. We are sowing, ev-er sowing, E'en in childhood's sunny
3. We are sowing, ev-er sowing, All thro' youth's bright summer
4. Still we're sowing, ev-er sowing, Till life's latest hour has

grain, And by day and night 'tis springing; Good and bad a-like are
hours, Seeds of love and peace and gladness, Or of sor-row, pain and
day: Oft with reckless hand we're flinging Germs that constantly are
flown; Let us then be ev-er care-ful, Ev-er watchful, ev-er

bring-ing Fruit we'll reap in joy or pain, Fruit we'll reap in joy or pain.
sad-ness, Yielding thorns or fra-grant flow'rs, Yielding thorns or fragrant flow'rs.
springing In-to life a-long our way, In-to life a-long our way.
pray'rful, For we'll reap as we have sown, For we'll reap as we have sown.

CHORUS.

We shall reap   as we sow,   Bit-ter fruit or golden grain;
We shall reap   as we sow,

We are Sowing.

We shall reap........ as we sow, Peace and joy, or grief and pain.
We shall reap as we sow,

No. 30. THE LORD LOOKS ON THE HEART.

M. S. SIBLEY.   (Old Tune "Rosefield.")   C. H. A. MALAN.

1. Tho' my home may hum-ble be,   Christ the Lord will sup with me;
2. Tho' my dress be worn and thin,   Joy-ful may I wel-come Him,
3. Tho' a mite be all my store,   Dives' gold can-not be more.
4. Let my gift be sweet with love;   Roy-al gift 'twill be a - bove.
5. Ab - ba, Fa - ther, I may pray,   Give Thy boun-ty day by day;

Poor and mea-ger be the fare,   It may prove a ban-quet rare;
Giv - ing all and of my best,   For He is a roy - al Guest.
Ere I spoke my needs He knew; "For His sake" the good I do;
Mer - cy show, since mer-cy's giv'n, Else how can I hope for heav'n?
Keep me ev - er in the right, Give me vic - t'ry in the fight,

Man sees but the out - ward part, But the Lord looks on the heart.
He will of His grace im - part, For the Lord looks on the heart.
Man may cause me keen-est smart, But the Lord looks on the heart.
Tho' I hold the high-est part, Still the Lord looks on the heart.
Since with wrong I have no part, For the Lord looks on the heart.

No. 31.   GOD IS WATCHING.

M. W. Snodgrass.

W. Irving Hartshorn. By per.

1. Oh, be care-ful, ev - er care-ful What you're choosing in your heart,
2. You would never, sure - ly nev - er, Turn a-way from this, His choice,
3. You would grieve at the re - fus - al Of His gift what-e'er it be,

Seek-ing this or that thing on - ly, Will-ing for no oth - er part.
Could you on - ly hear the of - fer In His ten - der, lov-ing voice.
Did you hear Him sad - ly say - ing, "But they have re - ject-ed me."

Chorus.

He is watch-ing, ev - er watching, Know-ing what is best for thee;

Then ac-cept it sweet-ly, glad - ly, What-so - ev - er it may be.

No. 32. FATHER, I HAVE HEARD THEE CALLING.

Eliza Sherman.　　　　　　　　　　　　W. Irving Hartshorn. By per.

Cantabile.

1. Fa-ther, I have heard Thee calling In sweet accents, "Come to me;"
2. In Thy lov-ing kindness, Father, All my tres-pass-es for-give
3. Oh, my Fa-ther, all un-wor-thy Am I of Thy ten-der-est love,

Ver-y far a-way I've wandered, But I'm com-ing now to Thee.
Je-sus, who hath died for sinners, Teach, oh, teach me how to live.
By which Thou wouldst draw Thy children To the heav'nly home a-bove.

CHORUS.

Fa-ther, Fa-ther, I am com-ing, Nev-er-more from Thee to roam,

While I hear Thy sweet voice calling, Father, I am coming home.

CHRIST IS ALL THE WORLD TO ME.

(Old Tune, "Annie Laurie.")　　　Arr. by T. M. T.

No. 33.

1. My soul is now u - nit - ed To Christ the living vine;
2. Soon as my love I gave Him, He pressed me to His breast,
3. He is my blest com-pan-ion, My sor-rows all are o'er,
4. I've tast-ed heav'nly pleasure, I need not fear a frown;

In lov - ing bonds I'm plight-ed,　To ev - er grow and twine.
My life in hap - py un - ion　With Him shall ev - er rest.
I've found a heav'n - ly por - tion,　'Tis joy for ev - er-more.
Christ is my joy and treas-ure,　My glo - ry and my crown.

CHORUS.

Christ is all the world to me, And His glo - ry I shall see,

And be fore I'd leave my Je - sus, I'd lay me down and die.

No. 34. ANGRY WORDS! OH, LET THEM NEVER.

Words and Music by Dr. H. R. PALMER.

1. An - gry words! oh, let them nev-er From the tongue un-bri-dled slip;
2. Love is much too pure and ho - ly; Friendship is too sa - cred far,
3. An - gry words are light-ly spok-en; Bitt'rest tho'ts are rash-ly stirred—

May the heart's best im-pulse ev - er Check them, ere they soil the lip.
For a moment's reck-less fol - ly Thus to des - o - late and mar.
Brightest links of life are bro-ken By a sin - gle an - gry word

CHORUS.

"Love one an - oth - er," Thus saith the Sav - ior, Children, o -
"Love each oth - er, love each oth - er,"

bey the Fa - ther's blest command: -bey His blest com - mand.
'Tis the Fa - ther's blest command: 'Tis His blest com - mand.

OME INTO THE LIGHT. ←———

D. C. C.

DAVID C. COOK.
Harmonized by T M. T.

1. Chil-dren of the light, why stay in the darkness,
2. Chil-dren of the light, Je-sus calls you to fol-low;
3. It will change your dullness to brightness and beauty;

No. 35.

Stumbling a-long in its gloom and night? Come to the light, it is
Darkness and night fade a-way at His sight; Pleasures a-wait, and a
E - ven the tear-drop shall glit-ter as gold; Shadows of earth shall

shin-ing so brightly, Come out of the darkness, come in - to the light.
bright crown of glo-ry, Leave all your fol-lies. Come in - to the light.
van - ish in noon-day, Warmth and com-fort exchange for your cold.

CHORUS.

Come in - to the light, Shining so bright, Shining for thee, for thee; It will

Come Into the Light.

brighten thy life, It will lighten its strife, It will fill thy soul with joy.

No. 36. **JUDGE NOT.**

FLORENCE McCARTHY. E B. SMITH. By per.

1, Cru - el   is the wound we give, Deep the harm our souls receive, By a
2. If   no one would make complaint, Till he were himself a saint, Love would
3. If   in cru - el haste we speak Of   the err - ing and the weak, We may
4. If   with lov-ing hearts we call On   the Fa - ther o - ver all, He will

word of heedless blame Cast upon an honest name: Judge not each other,
swiftly speed our way, Onward to a brighter day. Speak ev - er kind-ly,
feel the sting in turn, Till our own hearts ache and burn. Measure for measure,
hear each earnest prayer, He will make our cause His care. God hears His children,

judge not each other,   Judge not each other,   the Sav-ior tells us so.
speak ev - er kind-ly, Speak ev - er kind-ly, the Sav-ior tells us so.
meas - ure for measure, Meas - ure for measure, the Sav-ior tells us so.
God hears His children, God hears His children, the Sav-ior tells us so.

No. 37. SUNSHINE IN THE SOUL.

E. E. HEWITT.

JNO. R. SWENEY.

1. There's sunshine in my soul to-day, More glo - ri - ous and bright
2. There's mu-sic in my soul to-day, A car - ol to my King,
3. There's springtime in my soul to-day, For when the Lord is near,
4. There's gladness in my soul to-day, And hope and praise and love,

Than glows in an - y earth-ly sky, For Je - sus is my light.
And Je - sus, lis - ten-ing, can hear The songs I can - not sing.
The dove of peace sings in my heart, The flow'rs of grace ap - pear.
For blessings which He gives me now, For joys "laid up" a - bove.

REFRAIN.

Oh, there's sun - - - shine, Blessed sun - - - shine,
Oh, there's sunshine in the soul, Blessed sun-shine in the soul,

While the peace-ful, hap - py mo-ments roll; When
hap-py moments roll,

Je - sus shows His smil - ing face, There is sunshine in the soul.

No. 38. SHALL WE GATHER AT THE RIVER?

Rev. R. Lowry.

Cheerful.

1. Shall we gath-er at the riv-er Where bright an-gel feet have trod;
2. On the mar-gin of the riv-er, Wash-ing up its sil-ver spray,
3. On the bo-som of the riv-er, Where the Sav-ior-king we own,
4. Ere we reach the shining riv-er, Lay we ev-'ry bur-den down;

With its crys-tal tide for-ev - er Flow-ing by the throne of God?
We will walk and worship ev - er, All the hap-py, gold-en day.
We shall meet, and sor-row nev-er 'Neath the glo-ry of the throne.
Grace our spir-its will de-liv-er, And pro-vide a robe and crown.

CHORUS. *p*

Yes, we'll gather at the riv-er, The beautiful, the beautiful riv-er—

Gath-er with the saints at the riv-er That flows by the throne of God.

5 At the smiling of the river,
   Rippling with the Savior's face,
   Saints whom death will never sever
   Lift their songs of saving grace.

6 Soon we'll reach the shining river,
   Soon our pilgrimage will cease;
   Soon our happy hearts will quiver
   With the melody of peace.

BUCKLE ON THE SWORD

No. 39.

Rev. J. B. Atchinson.   W. S. Marshall. By per.

1. Broth - er, when you work for Je - sus, Buck - le on   the sword,
2. Broth - er, when you work for Je - sus, Keep your ar - mor bright,
3. Broth - er, when you work for Je - sus, Watch as well   as   pray,

En - e - mies are   all   a - round you, Buck - le on   the sword;
En - e - mies are   all   a - round you, Keep your ar - mor bright;
En - e - mies are   all   a - round you, Watch as well   as   pray;

Christ will give you wondrous pow'r, Give you vic - t'ry ev - 'ry hour,
Gird your-self a - bout with truth, Take with you the shield of faith,
Set   a watch both day and night, Pray in faith and work with might,

Make you more than con - quer - or. Buck - le on   the sword!
Would you con - quer sin and death, Keep your ar - mor bright!
Watch and pray and work and fight, Watch as well   as   pray!

No. 40. JESUS, I MY CROSS HAVE TAKEN.

HENRY F. LYTE.   MOZART.

1. Je - sus, I my cross have tak - en, All to leave and fol-low Thee;
2. Let the world despise and leave me, They have left my Sav-ior, too;
3. Go, then, earthly fame and treasure! Come, dis-as - ter, scorn and pain!
4. Haste thee on from grace to glory, Armed by faith and wing'd by pray'r:

Na - ked, poor, despised, for-sak-en, Thou, from hence, my all shalt be:
Human hearts and looks deceive me: Thou art   not, like man, un-true;
In Thy serv-ice, pain is pleasure: With Thy fa - vor, loss is gain.
Heav'n's e-ter-nal day's be-fore thee, God's own hand shall guide thee there.

Per - ish ev - 'ry fond am-bi-tion, All I've sought and hoped and known;
And while Thou shalt smile upon me, God   of wis-dom, love and might,
I have called Thee, "Abba, Fa-ther;" I have stayed my heart on Thee:
Soon shall close thy earthly mission, Swift shall pass thy pil-grim days;

Yet how rich is my con - di - tion, God and heav'n are still my own!
Foes may hate, and friends may shun me, Show Thy face and all is bright.
Storms may howl, and clouds may gather, All must work for good to me.
Hope shall change to glad fru-i - tion, Faith to sight, and prayer to praise.

LILY OF THE VALLEY. ✦

No. 41.

Arr. by T. M. T.

1. I've found a friend in Je-sus, He's ev-'ry-thing to me,
2. He all my griefs has tak-en, and all my sor-rows borne;
3. He'll nev-er, nev-er leave me, nor yet forsake me here,

He's the fair-est of ten thousand to my soul; The Lil-y
In temp-ta-tion He's my strong and mighty tow'r; I have all for
While I live by faith and do His bless-ed will; A wall of

D.S.—He's the Lil-y

of the Val-ley, in Him a-lone I see, All I need to cleanse and
Him for-sak-en, and all my i-dols torn From my heart, and now He
fire a-bout me, I've noth-ing now to fear; With His man-na He my

of the Val-ley, the bright and morning Star, He's the fair-est of ten

FINE.

keep me ful-ly whole; In sor-row He's my com-fort, in
keeps me by His power. Tho' all the world for-sake me, and
hun-gry soul shall fill; Then sweep-ing up to glo-ry we

thou-sand to my soul.

Lily of the Valley.

D.S.

troub-le He's my stay, He tells me ev - 'ry care on Him to roll,
Sa - tan tempts me sore, Thro' Je - sus I shall safe - ly reach the goal.
see His bless - ed face, Where riv - ers of de - light shall ev - er roll.

No. 42.   WORKING FOR HIM.

(Old Tune, "Cheer, Boys, Cheer.")   Arr. from RUSSEL,
by T. M. T.

ELLA ROCKWOOD.

1. Joy, sweet joy, to be the Lord's own help-er, Bear-ing the Gos - pel
2. Sweet, oh, sweet shall be the joy of working; Waiting up - on the
3. We would bear His Spir - it in our bosoms, Working without a

ti-dings on its way: Bless - ed in - deed to be a chos - en
Lord is our de - light; Glad - ly we toil, nor call the toil - ing
hope of earth-ly gain; Sure - ly e - nough to Him to be of

ves - sel, Fit for His use, tho' made of earth - ly clay.
la - bor; Heart joined with hand makes ev - 'ry la - bor light.
serv - ice, Giv - ing, we shall the best of all at - tain.

No. 43.   WONDERFUL LOVE.

Rev. J. B. Atchinson.   T. Martin Towne. By per.

1. 'Tis love, 'tis love, 'tis won-der-ful love! 'Twas God's great love for me,
2. 'Tis love, 'tis love, 'tis won-der-ful love! That fills my soul to-day:
3. 'Tis love, 'tis love, 'tis won-der-ful love! That cast-eth out all fear:
4. 'Tis love, 'tis love, 'tis won-der-ful love! Will take me home at last,

That sent the Sav-ior from a-bove, My sac-ri-fice to be!
'Tis love that fol-lows where I rove, That seeks me when I stray.
'Tis love that doth my song ap-prove, And whispers, " I am near."
To sing love's praise thro' endless days, When tri-als all are past.

CHORUS.

Won-der-ful, won-der-ful love,.......... Won-der-ful, won-der-ful,
won-der-ful love,

love,....... That sent the Sav-ior from above, My sac-ri-fice to be.
won-der-ful love,

No. 44.   TELL IT TO JESUS.

J. E. RANKIN, D. D.   E. S. LORENZ.

1. Are you wea - ry, are you heav - y-heart - ed? Tell it to Je - sus,
2. Do the tears flow down your cheeks unbidden? Tell it to Je - sus,
3. Do you fear the gath'ring clouds of sor - row? Tell it to Je - sus,
4. Are you troubled at the tho't of dy - ing? Tell it to Je - sus,

Tell it to Je - sus; Are you griev-ing o - ver joys de - part - ed?
Tell it to Je - sus; Have you sins that to man's eye are hid - den?
Tell it to Je - sus; Are you anx-ious what shall be to - mor-row?
Tell it to Je - sus; For Christ's coming Kingdom are you sigh-ing?

CHORUS.

Tell it to Je - sus a - lone. Tell it to Je - sus, tell it to Je - sus,

He is a friend that's well known: You have no oth - er

such a friend or broth - er, Tell it to Je - sus a - lone.

FROM "GATES OF PRAISE," BY PERMISSION OF E. S. LORENZ.

No. 45. SWEET MOUNT OF PRAYER.

ELLA McAFFERTY.　　　　　　FREDERIC H. PEASE. By per.

1. Out from the liv-ing tide, weary, oppressed, Calling His
2. When thro' the path of life, weary we stray, Je-sus with
3. Chos-en by such a friend, dearest and best, Ere we had

chosen ones, Jesus would rest; Rest from the pressing care, On that sweet mount of pray'r.
lov-ing voice, calls us away; How sweet to leave our care, And on the mount of pray'r,
tho't of Him, moments how blest! Taught at the mount of pray'r, Les-sons so rich and rare,

REFRAIN.

Whole nights He'd wrestled there, Blest, blest retreat! Blest, blest re-treat!
Meet with our Savior there, Blest, blest retreat!
Oh, to be oft-en there, Blest, blest retreat! Blest, blest retreat!

Blest, blest re-treat! Whole nights He'd wrestled there, Blest, blest re-treat!
Meet with our Savior there, Blest, blest re-treat!
Blest, blest retreat! Oh, to be oft-en there, Blest, blest re-treat!

No. 46. HAPPY GREETING.

Arranged.

1. Come, let us be joy-ful and min-gle our song, And hail the sweet
2. Dear Je-sus our Sav-ior, we lift up to Thee, Our voice of thanks-
3. And if, ere this new week has drawn to a close, Some loved one a-

joys which this day brings along; We'll join our glad voices in one hymn of praise
giv-ing, our glad ju-bi-lee; Protect us, and keep us, dear Je-sus, we pray,
mong us in death shall repose, O Lord, may the dear one in blessedness dwell,

CHORUS.

To Him who has kept us, and lengthened our days. Happy greeting to all!
That from Thy blest pre-cepts we never may stray
In the mansions of Jesus, where all shall be well. Happy greeting!

Happy greeting to all, Happy greeting, happy greeting, Happy greeting to all!

KIND WORDS CAN NEVER DIE

A. H.

ABBY HUTCHINSON.

No. 47.

1. { Kinds words can never die, Cherish'd and blest;
     God knows how deep they lie, Stor'd in the breast:
2. { Sweet thot's can never die, Tho', like the flow'rs,
     Their brightest hues may fly In win-try hours:
3. { Our souls can nev-er die, Tho' in the tomb
     We may all have to lie, Wrapp'd in its gloom.

Like childhood's simple rhymes, Said o'er a thousand times, Ay, in all
But when the gen-tle dew Gives them their charms anew, With many an
What tho' the flesh de-cay, Souls pass in peace a-way, Live thro' e-

years and climes, Dis-tant and near. Kind words can nev-er die,
add-ed hue They bloom a-gain. Sweet thot's can nev-er die,
ter-nal day With Christ a-bove. Our souls can nev-er die,

Nev-er die, nev-er die, Kind words can never die, No, nev-er die.
Nev-er die, nev-er die, Sweet thot's can never die, No, nev-er die.
Nev-er die, nev-er die, Our souls can never die, No, nev-er die.

No. 48. IS NOT THIS THE LAND OF BEULAH?

Anon.   Arranged.

1. I am dwell-ing on the mountain, Where the gold-en sun-light gleams,
2. I can see far down the mountain, Where I wandered wea - ry years,
3. I am drink-ing at the fount-ain, Where I ev - er would a - bide;

O'er a land whose wondrous beauty Far ex-ceeds my fondest dreams;
Oft - en hin-dered in my jour-ney By the ghosts of doubts and fears;
For I've tast - ed life's sweet riv - er, And my soul is sat - is - fied;

Where the air is pure, e - the-real, La-den with the breath of flow'rs,
Bro - ken vows and disappointments Thick-ly sprinkled all the way,
There's no thirsting for life's pleasures, Nor a-dorn - ing rich and gay,

Cho.—*Is not this the land of Beu-lah, Bless-ed, bless - ed land of light,*

D.S. Chorus.

They are blooming by the fountain, 'Neath the am - a - ranth-ine bow'rs.
But the Spir - it led, un - err - ing, To the land I hold to - day.
For I've found a rich - er treas-ure, One that fad - eth not a - way.

Where the flow - ers bloom for-ev - er, And the sun is al-ways bright.

No. 49.   SWEET BY-AND-BY.

S. FILLMORE BENNETT.   JOS. P. WEBSTER.

1. There's a land that is fair - er than day, And by faith we can see it a-
2. We shall sing on that beau-ti-ful shore The mel - o - di - ous songs of the
3. To our boun-ti - ful Fa-ther a - bove, We will of - fer our trib - ute of

far; For the Fa-ther waits o - ver the way, To pre-pare us a
blest, And our spir - its shall sor-row no more, Not a sigh for the
praise, For the glo - ri - ous gift of His love, And the bless-ings that

CHORUS.

dwelling place there. In the sweet   by-and-by,   We shall
bless-ing of rest.
hal - low our days.   In the sweet   by-and-by,

meet on that beau-ti-ful shore,   In the sweet   by-and-
by-and-by,   by-and-by,

Sweet By-and=By.

by, (by - and - by.) We shall meet on that beau - ti - ful shore.

No. 50.

No. 51.

1 From Greenland's icy mountains,
   From India's coral strand:
   Where Afric's sunny fountains
   Roll down their golden sand;
   From many an ancient river,
   From many a palmy plain,
   They call us to deliver
   Their land from error's chain.

2 What though the spicy breezes
   Blow soft o'er Ceylon's isle;
   Though every prospect pleases,
   And only man is vile?
   In vain with lavish kindness
   The gifts of God are strown;
   The heathen in his blindness
   Bows down to wood and stone.

3 Shall we, whose souls are lighted
   With wisdom from on high,
   Shall we to men benighted
   The lamp of life deny?
   Salvation! O salvation!
   The joyful sound proclaim,
   Till earth's remotest nation
   Has learned Messiah's name.

4 Waft, waft, ye winds, His story,
   And you, ye waters, roll,
   Till like a sea of glory,
   It spreads from pole to pole;
   Till o'er our ransomed nature
   The Lamb for sinners slain,
   Redeemed, King, Creator,
   In bliss returns to reign.

1 In the secret of His presence,
   I am kept from strife of tongues,
   His pavilion is around me,
   And within are ceaseless songs;
   Stormy winds, His words fulfilling,
   Beat without, but cannot harm,
   For the Master's voice is stilling
   Storm and tempest to a calm.

2 In the secret of His presence,
   All the darkness disappears,
   For a sun that knows no setting,
   Throws a rainbow on my tears;
   So the day grows ever brighter,
   Broadening to the perfect noon,
   So the way grows ever brighter,
   Heaven is coming near and soon.

3 In the secret of His presence,
   Nevermore can foes alarm;
   In the shadow of the highest,
   I can meet them with a song:
   For the strong pavilion hides me,
   Turns their fiery darts aside,
   And I know whate'er betides me,
   I shall live because He died.

4 In the secret of His presence,
   In the sweet, unbroken rest,
   Pleasures, joys, in glorious fullness,
   Making earth like Eden blest:
   So my peace grows deep and deeper,
   Widening as it nears the sea,
   For my Savior is my keeper,
   Keeping mine and keeping me.

Rev. HENRY BURTON.

SEEKING FOR ME.
No. 52.

E. E. H.

E. E. HASTY.

1. Jesus, my Savior, to Bethlehem came, Born in a manger to
2. Jesus, my Savior, on Calvary's tree, Suffer'd and died, and my
3. Jesus, my Savior, the same as of old, While I did wander a-

sor-row and shame, Oh, it was won-der-ful, blest be His name, Seeking for me,
soul He set free; Oh, it was won-der-ful, how could it be? Dy-ing for me,
far from the fold, Gently and long He hath plead with my soul, Calling for me,

for me,........ for me,........

for me, Seeking for me, seeking for me, Seeking for me, seeking for me:
for me, Dying for me, dy-ing for me, Dy-ing for me, dy-ing for me:
for me, Calling for me, calling for me, Calling for me, calling for me:

Oh, it was won-der-ful, blest be His name, Seeking for me, for me.
Oh, it was won-der-ful, how could it be? Dy-ing for me, for me.
Gently and long He hath plead with my soul, Calling for me, for me.

FROM "GOOD WILL," BY PER. OF TOWNE & STILLMAN.

No. 53. YIELD NOT TO TEMPTATION.

Words and Music by H. R. PALMER.

1. Yield not to temp-ta-tion, For yielding is sin,   Each vic-t'ry will
2. Shun e - vil com-pan-ions, Bad language dis-dain, God's name hold in
3. To him that o'ercometh God giv-eth a   crown, Thro' faith we shall

help you Some oth - er to   win; Fight man-ful - ly on - ward,
rev - 'rence, Nor take it in   vain; Be thoughtful and earn - est,
con - quer, Though oft -en cast down; He who is our Sav - ior,

Dark passions sub-due, Look ev - er to Je-sus, He'll car-ry you through.
Kind-hearted and true, Look ev - er to Je-sus, He'll car-ry you through.
Our strength will renew, Look ev - er to Je-sus, He'll car-ry you through.

CHORUS.

Ask the Sav - ior to help you, Com-fort, strengthen, and keep you;

He is will-ing to aid you, He will car - ry you through.

No. 54. CLIMB A LITTLE LONGER.

FANNIE E. TOWNSLEY. T. M. TOWNE. By per.

DUET. **CHORUS.**

1. Trav'ler, tho' your feet are worn, Climb a lit-tle long-er;
2. Tho' your heart is aching sore, Bear a lit-tle long-er;
3. Step by step climb higher still, Climb a lit-tle long-er;
4. Glo-ry in the sunset land Waits a lit-tle long-er;

DUET. **CHORUS.**

Tho' with thorns your hands are torn, Climb a lit-tle long-er.
Stands an-oth-er cross be-fore? Lift a lit-tle long-er.
At the top your heart shall thrill, Help a lit-tle long-er.
Till the loved shall clasp your hand With a love grown strong-er.

Thorns shall change to waving palms, Tempests cease in heav'nly calms,
No more heart-ache, no more pain, In the land you yet shall gain,
On your brow shall shine a gem, Sparkling in life's di-a-dem,
Friends are beck'ning from the skies, Urg-ing on the soul that tries

Joy shall ban-ish your a-larms, Wait a lit-tle long-er.
On-ly faith-ful-ly re-main True a lit-tle long-er.
In the new Je-ru-sa-lem On, a lit-tle long-er.
Still to reach heav'n's par-a-dise, On, a lit-tle long-er.

No. 55. MY HEART SHALL BE A TEMPLE.

Rev. H. B. Hartzler. W. F. Sherwin. By per.

1 My heart shall be a tem - ple For Thee, my gra-cious Lord;
2. My heart shall be a tem - ple, A con - se - crat - ed place,
3. My heart shall be a tem - ple All fit - ted up for Thee,

I hear Thy friendly sum - mons, I o - pen at Thy word.
Il - lu-mined by Thy glo - ry, The shin - ing of Thy face.
That Thou may'st come and sup, Lord, With me, and I with Thee.

CHORUS.

My heart shall be a tem - ple, Pre-pared for Thee a - lone,

I pray Thee, come and en - ter, And make it all Thine own.

No. 56.   REMEMBER THY CREATOR.

(Old Tune, "We'd Better Bide a Wee.")   CLARIBEL.

Rev. ROBT. KERR.

Arr. by T. M. T.

1. Re-mem-ber Him in youthful days, Who gave thee life and breath,
2. Re-mem-ber Him in life's fresh hour, So beau - ti - ful and bright,
3. Re-mem-ber Him who free - ly left The heights of bliss a - bove,

Whose mercy crowns thee, and whose pow'r Redeems thee still from death;
Be-fore old age shall bring the days That yield thee no de - light;
And died for us, that we might live, And give Him love for love;

Re - mem-ber, oh, re-mem-ber Him, Whose goodness follows thee,
Re - mem-ber, oh, re-mem-ber Him, Whose heart so yearns to see
Re - mem-ber, oh, re-mem-ber Him, Who died up - on the tree,

And let His serv - ice and His love Thy con-stant glo - ry be,
Thy soul o'er-flow with pur - est joy, And seeks to dwell with thee,
And when in glo - ry He ap-pears, He will re - mem - ber thee,

Remember Thy Creator.

And let His serv-ice and His love Thy con-stant glo - ry be.
Thy soul o'er-flow with pur-est joy, And seeks to dwell with thee.
And when in glo - ry He ap-pears, He will re - mem - ber thee.

No. 57. JOYFULLY CONFESS HIM.

M. W. SNODGRASS.   T. MARTIN TOWNE. By per.

1. Sing, if you love your Savior, Tell of His love, "Chiefest among ten
2. Love that is worth confessing, Grows in-to deeds, Sow words and works to-
3. Stand with the church of Jesus; Bravely de-clare You are the Lord's dis-
4. Then, as the Master's servant More workers call; Tell them the fields are

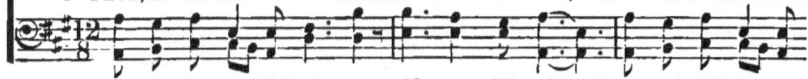

D.C.—*Stand, and you will be stronger, Close to His side, Once under God's pro-*

CHORUS.

thou-sand," All else a - bove.
geth - er, Like choic - est seeds.
ci - ple, True ev - 'ry - where.   } Joy - ful - ly now confess Him,
white with Har - vest for all.

tec - tion, Naught can be - tide.

D.C.

Stand tho' a - lone, An-gels de-light to bless Him, Low at His throne;

No. 58.

D. C. C.

DAVID C. COOK.
Harmonized by T. M. T.

1. Have you heard of the won-der-ful Je - sus, The light of the
2. Have you heard how He loved the chil - dren? How He fold-ed them
3. Have you heard how He wept at Bethany, In their sad be-

world a - bove; How He came to a world of sor - row To
to His breast? Of His call to the wea - ry - heart-ed, With its
reavement hour, How He gave them back their broth-er, In His

tell of the Fa-ther's love? He is just the same as then, to-day,
promise of peace and rest? He is just the same as then, to-day,
wou - drous love and power? He is just the same as then, to-day,

He is just the same as then; With His love and light, He would
He is just the same as then; In His strong arms of love, He would
He is just the same as then; He would call from the tomb All its

He is Just the Same as Then.

en - ter thy soul, He would make thy life all bright.
car - ry His child, And bear to the home a - bove.
bur - - ied hopes To jew - el thy heav'n - ly home.

4 Have you heard how He stilled the
tempest,
How He made the sea at rest,
How He cast out the fierce demoniac,
How He calmed each troubled breast?
He is just the same as then, to-day,
He is just the same as then;
He will speak "peace, be still"
To thy storm-tossed soul,
If you yield it to His will.

5 Have you heard of His conquest at
Calvary.
Of His grand triumphant cry?
It is glorious to live as the Savior lived,
It is grander still to die;
He is just the same as then, to day,
He is just the same as then;
He would bear you aright,
Through your trials here,
You may triumph by His might.

No. 59.   MANY MANSIONS.

E. A. BARNES.   A. J. ABBEY. By per.

1. Ma-ny man-sions far a - bove, Ev - er bright with joy and love,
2. Not a morn that has its night, Not a day that bringeth blight,
3. Not a grave shall there ap - pear, Not a mourner's bit - ter tear,
4. Not a life that grow-eth old, Not a death with - in that fold;

Not a grief shall en - ter there, Not a tri - al, not a care.
Not a fate which oft be - reaves, Not a soul that sad - ly grieves.
Not a sigh from trouble born, Not a rose that has its . thorn.
Ma-ny mansions bright and free; Brother, is there one for thee?

No. 60. SINGING ON.

Rev. C. R. Pattee.　　　　　　　　C. E. Pollock.　By per.

1. Singing on a-mid the sunshine, Yearning not for days of yore.
2. Trusting on a-mid the darkness, Looking for the farther shore.
3. Hoping on a-mid the con-flict, When the battle rages sore.
4. Shouting on a-mid death's waters, Heeding not their sullen roar,

All my path　a　scene of glad-ness, Shining brightest on　be - fore;
Calmly wait - ing　for the morn-ing, When the shadows shall be　o'er;
Tho' the heart, all crush'd and breaking, Wounded, bleeds at ev - 'ry　pore;
Shouting back　in　ho - ly　tri - umph, From the ev - er-bless - ed　shore;

Singing ev - er, sigh-ing nev - er, And re - joic - ing　ev - er-more;
Trusting ev - er, doubt-ing nev - er, And re - joic - ing　ev - er-more;
Hop-ing ev - er, yield-ing nev - er, And re - joic - ing　ev - er-more;
Shouting ev - er, fear-ing nev - er, And re - joic - ing　ev - er-more:

Singing　ev - er, sigh-ing nev - er, And re - joic-ing ev - er - more.
Trusting　ev - er, doubt-ing nev - er, And re - joic-ing ev - er - more.
Hop-ing　ev - er, yield-ing nev - er, And re - joic-ing ev - er - more.
Shouting ev - er, fear-ing nev - er, And re - joic-ing ev - er - more.

No. 61. WHAT ARE YOU GOING TO DO?

E. A. HOFFMAN.   E. B. SMITH. By per.

1. Je - sus is call-ing and bids you re-turn. Why will you long-er His
2. Boundless in mer - cy, in - vit - ing He stands, Bearing a par-don with-
3. Oft - en re - ject - ed, He comes yet a-gain, When will you love and ac-
4. Life is re - ced - ing and ebb - ing a - way, Why will you long-er from
5. Christ is most ten-der - ly call - ing to you; Brother, oh, what are you
6. Why not ac-cept Him whose love is so great, Ere you shall find it for-

CHORUS.

mer · cy spurn? ⎫
in His hands. ⎪
cept Him—when? ⎬ Je - sus is wait-ing, wait - ing, wait - ing,
Je- · sus stay? ⎪
go - ing to do? ⎪
ev · er too late? ⎭

Christians are fer-vent-ly pray - ing for you; While yet the door of sweet

mer - cy is o - pen, Broth - er, oh, what are you go-ing to do?

No. 62. NO FRIEND LIKE JESUS.

A. W. H.   A. W. Hare.

1. There's no friend like Je - sus, so won-drous-ly kind, No friend like my
2. There's no friend like Je - sus, in Him I a - bide, And find His com-
3. There's no friend like Je - sus, He's ev - er the same, So gen - tle and

Sav - ior for me; More joy than in all else in Je - sus I find,
pan - ion-ship sweet, My joy and my sor - row to Him I con-fide,
lov - ing and true; Oh, trust in His prom-ise, be-lieve on His name,

Chorus.

Thro' Je - sus a - lone I am free.
And in Him find com-fort com-plete. } There's no friend like Je-sus, Oh,
There's no friend like Je - sus for you.

trust Him to-day, A friend un-to sin-ners is He; Your sins He will

par - don, your guilt take a-way, And Je-sus your best friend will be.

No. 63. PRAISE, PRAISE TO JESUS.

DAVID C. COOK.   L. E. JONES.

1. Bright is the pil - grim way, Leads on to end - less day,
2. Glad is the praise we bring, Oh, let us ev - er sing,
3. Soon in the hap - py land, With all the blest to stand,

From it we would not stray; He leads us on, He is our
Ev - er on joy-ous wing, Praise, praise to Him; Loud let the
With all the white-robed band, Dwell, dwell for aye, Hap - py at

CHORUS.

staff and stay, He leads us on.
anthems ring, Praise, praise to Him. } Praise, praise to Jesus, Praise, praise to
His right hand, Dwell, dwell for aye. }

Je - sus, Loud let our anthems ring; Praise, praise to Him.

NOT AS I WILL

No. 64.

DAVID C. COOK.

T. MARTIN TOWNE.

1. Not as I will, dear Christ, Not as I will: Thy will is
2. Al - ways the jour - ney sweet, Close by Thy side; Be - neath Thy
3. Not as I will, dear Christ, In bit - ter pain; Best is the
4. Best, it is al - ways so, Thou know-est best; Trust - ing Thy

ev - er best, Thy will be done.
bless - ed will My will to hide.
cup for me, Ev - er my gain.
lov - ing care, In Thee I rest.

CHORUS.

Ev - er my prayer shall be,

Not as I will, For on - ly as Thou wilt Is best for me.

No. 65. Blest be the Tie.

1 Blest be the tie that binds
  Our hearts in Christian love;
The fellowship of kindred minds
  Is like to that above.

2 Before our Father's throne,
  We pour our ardent prayers;
Our fears, our hopes, our aims are one,
Our comforts and our cares.

3 We share our mutual woes;
  Our mutual burdens bear;
And often for each other flows
  The sympathizing tear.

4 When we asunder part,
  It gives us inward pain;
But we shall still be joined in heart,
  And hope to meet again,

No. 66. THE BEATITUDES.

Rev. W. Wye Smith.   W. F. Sherwin. By per.

1. Bless-ed! bless-ed! Poor in spir - it, Mourning, weeping on the way;
2. Bless-ed! bless-ed! Meek and low-ly, You from strife and rage a - far;
3. Bless-ed! bless-ed! Hung'ring, thirsting, For the righteousness you love;
4. Bless-ed! bless-ed! Kind, for-giv-ing, In the smile of God you rest;

Yours a king-dom to in - her - it, God shall wipe your tears a - way.
Earth is yours and heav'n so ho - ly, You shall shine where angels are.
Lo for you the Fount is burst-ing, And the feast a-waits a - bove.
Mer-cy from on high re - ceiv - ing, Bless-ed now and ev - er blest.

Chorus.

Bless - ed, bless-ed! O pure heart-ed And who make and live for peace;

You from God shall ne'er be part-ed, Nor from you his fa - vor cease.

HE FIRST LOVED ME

Arranged.
Animated.

CHAS. EDW. POLLOCK.

No. 67.

1. May I learn from day to day, Love's sweet lesson to o-bey;
2. With a joyous heart of love, At Thy bidding may I move,
3. So may I rejoice to show That I feel the love I owe,

Sweet-er les-son can-not be, Lov-ing Him who first loved me.
Prompt to trust and fol-low Thee, Lov-ing Him who first loved me.
Sing-ing till that face I see, Lov-ing Him who first loved me.

CHORUS

Lov-ing Him who first loved me, Lov-ing Him who first loved me;

None so pre-cious half can be, Take the love I bring to Thee.

No. 68. DO THE DUTY LYING NEAREST.

CARRIE WRIGHT.   F. W. TIDBALL. By per.

1. Seek not for some far - off mis-sion, Un-done work is close at hand;
2. Op - por-tu - ni - ties will greet thee, On - ly watch with greatest care;
3. All the need-ed help He'll give thee, Tho' He work or tri - als send;

Wait not for some glorious vis - ion, Al-most com-ing with com-mand.
Something brave to do, it may be, Or, per-haps, something to bear.
On - ly trust and love Him al-ways, Serv-ing faith-ful to the end.

CHORUS.

Do the du - ty ly - ing near-est, E - ven tho' it hum-ble be,

There may come some priceless blessing, Lasting as e - ter - ni - ty.

No. 69. JESUS, KEEP ME.

DAVID C. COOK.   M. VILLA.

1. Dear Je-sus, keep me ev - er with thy - self; Life with - out Thee
2. O Je-sus, ev - er jour - ney by my side, Let me feel Thy
3. O Je-sus, be en-thron'd within my soul May my tho'ts and

now is . los - ing all its charms. I have found in Thee the
pres-ence with me all the way. Let me hear Thy words of
words flow ev - er forth from Thee Keep me cleans'd and pure from

source of life and light, Thy blest presence scatters all a - larms.
coun-sel and of love, Hap - py to be with Thee all the day.
ev - 'ry stain of siu, Ev - er - more a - bid - ing may I be.

CHORUS.

Yes, Je-sus, hold me closely in Thine arms, Ev - er round me may they

be, Till in the sunshine of Thy love, I shall rest e-ter - nal - ly.

No. 70.   I WILL ARISE.

J. E. H.   J. E. HALL. By per.

1. I will a-rise and go to my Fa-ther, For He will sure-ly
2. I will a-rise; oh, why should I tar - ry, Liv - ing this life so
3. I will a-rise; 'tis fol - ly to lin - ger, For I grow sin-ful

let me come in; Tho' of His love I am so un-wor-thy,
mean and so low, Eat-ing these husks which sat - is - fy nev - er?
while here I stay; Soon it may be too late home to en - ter,

CHORUS.

He will for-give me, free - ly, my sin.)
Filled is my heart with sor - row and woe. } I will a - rise,
And I for - ev - er must stay a - way.)

I will a - rise, And seek my Fa-ther's face with-out de - lay;

I will a-rise, I will a - rise, Here in my sins I'll no longer stay.

LET US KEEP THE GOLDEN RULE

BESSIE L. BARTLETT.　　　　　　　　T. MARTIN TOWNE.

No. 71.

1. There's a measure for us all, Good for home or school;
2. Judg-ing oth-ers is a sin That we all should shun;
3. If we judge. we shall be judged, That is ver-y true;
4. Then a-mid life's bat-tle wild, Let us still keep cool,

One we nev-er should de-spise, For 'tis the Gold-en Rule.
For we can-not see the heart To tell why things are done.
Then treat oth-ers just the way That you'd have them treat you.
Show-ing oth-ers, day by day, The bless-ed Gold-en Rule.

CHORUS.

Do-ing then to oth-ers, As we'd have them do:

Let us keep the Gold-en Rule, He will help us to......

No. 72. BEHOLD THE LOVE.

E. M. CLARK.   Mrs. MORTON. By per.

1. Be - hold the love, the boundless love, The love be-yond   de - gree;
2. E'en when I walked the paths of sin, And spurned His love so   true,

In - fi - nite love in Christ displayed, From God thro' Christ to me.
He loved me still; so much He loved, To   die He dared to   do;

No earth - ly friend e'er loved so well, So   deep, so con-stant - ly;
Though lost in darkness and in doubt, And bruised and stained with sin,

Or loved when love was not re-turned, As Christ my Lord loved me.
Though earth-ly friends re - fuse to know, He'll wel - come us to Him.

No. 73. IN THE PATH I'M WALKING.

Rev. J. B. ATCHINSON.   J. W. BISCHOFF. By per.

1. { In the path I'm walking, Pleasant is the way,
   { Oh, I love this highway, Pathway of the just,

2. { In this pleas-ant pathway, Walking will not tire,
   { Blessed are the pil-grims, Walking in this way,

Each day grow-ing brighter, Till the per-fect day;
[Omit. . . . .] Christ is my com-
Run-ning will not wea-ry, As we mount up higher;
[Omit. . . . .] Shin-ing more and

pan - ion,   In Him I will trust. }
bright - er, Till the per - fect day. } In this bless-ed path - way,

Christ is my delight, Hand in hand we jour-ney Tow'rd the realms of light.

CHORUS.

No. 74.   JESUS IS WITH ME.

DAVID C. COOK.
D. C. C.   Harmonized by T. M. T.

1. Sweet is the jour-ney, bright is the way, Leading me on to the
2. Oh, to be ev - er close by His side, Un-der His love all my

mansions of day, Tho'ts of His pres-ence fill me with cheer: I am so
wor-ries to hide, Knowing He al - ways does what is best, Trusting and

CHORUS.

hap - py to have Je - sus here.)
lov - ing I'm al - ways at rest. ʃ Je-sus is with me, Je-sus is

with me, Sweet-est com-mun-ion with Him all the way. Oh, how He

loves me; oh, how I love Him, Je-sus, dear Je - sus, is with me all day.

No. 75. TAKE MY HAND.

Rev. E. A. HOFFMAN   C. E. POLLOCK. By per.

1. With my hand in that of Je-sus, I would joy-ful, joy-ful be,
2. With my hand in that of Je-sus, I will trust-ful, trust-ful be,

Tho' the clouds hang dark and heavy, And the way I can-not see;
I will be con-tent and hap-py, Knowing He will care for me;

For the Lord will safe-ly lead me Thro' the dark-ness in-to light;
Should all earth-ly friends for-sake me, Should all earth-ly joys de-part,

In His own good time and pleas-ure, He will make my pathway bright.
I will still be calm and joy-ful, I will trust-ful be of heart.

CHORUS.

Take my hand, O bless-ed Je-sus! Guide me thro' this world of care!

Take My Hand.

Bring me to the heav'nly mansions, To en - joy the glo - ry there.

No. 76.

1 I was a wandering sheep,
  I did not love the fold:
I did not love my Shepherd's voice,
  I would not be controlled;
I was a wayward child,
  I did not love my home,
I did not love my Father's voice,
  I loved afar to roam.

2 The Shepherd sought His sheep,
  The Father sought His child;
They followed me o'er vale and hill,
  O'er deserts waste and wild;
They found me nigh to death,
  Famished and faint and lone;
They bound me with the bands of love,
  They saved the wandering one.

3 Jesus my Shepherd is,
  'Twas He that loved my soul;
'Twas He that saved me by His life,
  'Twas He that made me whole;
'Twas He that sought the lost,
  That found the wandering sheep,
'Twas He that brought me to the fold,
  'Tis He that still doth keep.

No. 77.

1 Savior, like a Shepherd lead us,
  Much we need Thy tenderest care;
In Thy pleasant pastures feed us,
  For our use Thy folds prepare.
Blessed Jesus, blessed Jesus,
  Thou hast bought us, Thine we are;
Blessed Jesus, blessed Jesus,
  Thou hast bought us, Thine we are.

2 We are Thine, do Thou befriend us,
  Be the Guardian of our way;
Keep Thy flock, from sin defend us,
  Seek us when we go astray
Blessed Jesus, blessed Jesus,
  Hear Thy children when they pray,
Blessed Jesus, blessed Jesus,
  Hear Thy children when they pray.

3 Early let us seek Thy favor,
  Early let us do Thy will;
Blessed Lord and only Savior,
  With Thy love our bosoms fill.
Blessed Jesus, blessed Jesus,
  Thou hast loved us, love us still,
Blessed Jesus, blessed Jesus,
  Thou hast loved us, love us still.

HE IS WITH ME

No. 78.

D. C. C.

DAVID C. COOK.

Harmonized by T. M. T.

1. Worlds on worlds are in His keep-ing, Yet He keeps me by His pow'r;
2. Love di-vine is o'er me steal-ing, Love un-meas-ured all the way;
3. If with-in the den of li - ons, I may know His matchless grace,
4. If with-in the fier - y fur-nace I may see His bless-ed face,
5. He has pow'r o'er storm and tempest, He has pow'r o'er sin and strife;

Day and night He knows no sleep-ing, He is with me ev - 'ry hour.
Love that makes earth's pris-on, pal-ace, Love that makes earth's night all day.
With His an - gel watch-ing o'er me, I shall laugh, their pow'r to face.
Sweetest mo-ments then life's tri-als, Bless-ed trophies of His grace.
Glad with Him to sail life's o - cean, In His keep-ing trust my life

CHORUS.

Ev - 'ry hour He is most pre-cious, Ev - 'ry day He is my stay;

Noth-ing e'er can come to hurt me, He is with me all the way.

No. 79. MAY I CLOSER GROW TO THEE.

M. W. SNODGRASS.   T. M. TOWNE   By per.

1 Je - sus, Thou art ev - er love - ly, Thou the true and beauteous Vine!
2. As the branch cannot be fruit-ful, Severed from the liv-ing vine,
3. If there be this sa-cred nearness, Then the springing life will glow;

Un - to Thee my soul's af - fec-tions Ev - er seek to turn and twine.
So my life is dead and worthless If it be not one with Thine.
Then the love will warm and rip-en, And the fruit-ful clus-ters grow.

CHORUS.

Ev - 'ry day, Lord, I pray, May I clos - er grow to Thee;

As the branch to the vine, May the bless - ed un - ion be.

IF I WERE A SUNBEAM.

LUCY LARCOM.

T. M. TOWNE.

No. 80.

1. If I were a sun-beam, I know what I would do;
2. If I were a sun-beam, I know where I would go;
3. Art thou not a sun-beam, O child whose heart is glad,

I'd seek the whit - est lil - y   The rain - y woodland through;
In - to the low - liest hov - els,   All dark with want and woe;
With still an in - ner ra-diance   That sun-shine nev - er   had.

Steal - ing in   a - mong them, The soft - est light I'd shed,
Till sad hearts looked up - ward, I   then would shine and shine!
As the Lord hath blessed thee, Oh, scat - ter rays di - vine,

Un - til each grace-ful lil - y   Raised its droop - ing head.
Then they would think of heav - en,   Their sweet home and mine.
For there can be no sun-beam,   But must die or shine.

No. 81.   SONG OF SUNSHINE.

E. B. Smith. By per.

1. Be con - tent with what you have, Life at best is shad - ed;
2. Do not think your lot is hard, Cheer-less like De - cem - ber,
3. Try to do some act of love, Try some heart to glad - den;
4. Nothing like a cheer-ful heart Frightens care and sor - row;

Seek the sun-shine while it lasts, Ere its light is fad - ed.
Some one's lot is hard - er yet, Al - ways that re - mem - ber.
While that heart you're binding up, Yours will nev - er sad - den.
Noth - ing like a beam-ing face Can the sun - light bor - row.

CHORUS.

Be con - tent, be con - tent, Skies will bright-en o'er you,

Be con-tent with what you have, Bet - ter days be - fore you.

No. 82.

DO IT TO=DAY.

O. D. SHERMAN.

J. M. STILLMAN.

1. If we on - ly knew what good we could do, In this
2. An - y cheer - ing word, in gloom that is heard, By a
3. And a lov - ing smile, some heart may in - cline To the

world of sin and sor - row, We would not de - lay, but
heart that grief would bor - row, May light - en the load, and
path that's straight and nar - row; A kind, friend-ly deed to

do it to - day, And nev - er wait for to - mor - row, No,
bright - en the road; So nev - er wait for to - mor - row, No,
one in his need Is bet - ter now than to - mor - row, Yes,

nev - er wait for to-mor - row, No, nev - er wait for to-mor - row; But
nev - er wait for to-mor - row, No, nev - er wait for to-mor - row; But
bet - ter now than to-mor-row, Yes, bet - ter now than to-mor - row; So,

FROM "GOOD WILL," BY PERMISSION OF TOWNE & STILLMAN.

Do It To-day.

do it to-day, and nev - er de-lay, And save a world of sor-row.
speak it to day, and nev - er de-lay, 'Twill lift the clouds of sor-row.
do it to-day, and nev - er de-lay, And save a world of sor-row

No. 83.

No. 84.

1 Work, for the night is coming,
  Work through the morning hours:
Work, while the dew is sparkling,
  Work 'mid springing flowers;
Work, when the day grows brighter,
  Work in the glowing sun;
Work, for the night is coming,
  When man's work is done.

2 Work, for the night is coming,
  Work through the sunny noon:
Fill brightest hours with labor,
  Rest comes sure and soon.
Give every flying minute
  Something to keep in store:
Work, for the night is coming,
  When man works no more.

3 Work, for the night is coming,
  Under the sunset skies:
While their bright tints are glowing.
  Work, for daylight flies.
Work, till the last beam fadeth,
  Fadeth to shine no more:
Work while the night is darkening,
  When man's work is o'er.

1 Love divine, all love excelling,
  Joy of heaven, to earth come down!
Fix in us Thy humble dwelling;
  All Thy faithful mercies crown.
Jesus, Thou art all compassion,
  Pure, unbounded love Thou art;
Visit us with Thy salvation;
  Enter every trembling heart.

2 Breathe.oh, breathe Thy loving Spirit
  Into every troubled breast!
Let us all in Thee inherit,
  Let us find that second rest.
Take away our bent to sinning;
  Alpha and Omega be:
End of faith, as its beginning,
  Set our hearts at liberty.

3 Finish then Thy new creation;
  Pure and spotless let us be;
Let us see Thy great salvation
  Perfectly restored in Thee:
Changed from glory into glory,
  Till in heaven we take our place,
Till we cast our crowns before Thee:
  Lost in wonder, love and praise.

WALKING WITH GOD.
No. 85.

D. C. C.

DAVID C. COOK.

Harmonized by T. M. T.

1. Walking with God, walking with God; Higher His ways than the
2. Walking with God, walking with God, Out of attractions of
3. Walking with God, walking with God, Far, far a-bove earth's

heav-ens are, Far, far away from earth's vain care, Walking, walking with God.
earth complete, Sheltered and loved in His retreat. Walking, walking with God.
clouds and storms, Where nothing comes that hurts or harms, Walking, walking with God.

CHORUS.

Walking with God by night and day; Walking with God the star-ry way;

Walking with Him e - ter - nal - ly, Walking, walking with God.

No. 86.   I'LL STAND BY MY SCHOOL.

BELLE KELLOGG TOWNE.   T. MARTIN TOWNE.

Moderato.

1. I'll pledge my heart, I'll pledge my hand, Beside my Sunday School to stand,
2. I'll pledge my heart, I'll pledge my hand, Beside my Sunday School to stand,
3. I'll pledge my heart, I'll pledge my hand, Beside my Sunday School to stand,
4. I'll pledge my heart, I'll pledge my hand, Beside my Sunday School to stand,

Its les-sons I will learn with care, And in its du-ties ev-er share,
From day to day, from week to week, The truths it teach-es, I will seek.
And of-fi-cers and teach-ers kind In me a help-er true shall find.
Nor will I tempt-ed be to roam From this my pleasant Sabbath home.

CHORUS.

This pledge I will take, my life by it rule, God be-ing my help-er, I'll stand by my school,

Cres.   *ff*   *Rit.*

I'll stand by my school, I'll stand by my school, God be-ing my help-er, I'll stand by my school.

JESUS, THE LIGHT OF THE WORLD.

G. D. E. Arr.   GEO. D. ELDERKIN. Arr.

No. 87.

1. Hark! the Her-ald angels sing, Jesus, the Light of the world:
2. Joy - ful all ye nations rise, Jesus, the Light of the world:
3. Christ by highest heav'n adored, Jesus, the Light of the world;
4. Hail! the heav'n-born Prince of peace, Jesus, the Light of the world;

Glo - ry to the new-born King, Je-sus, the Light of the world.
Join the tri-umphs of the skies, Je-sus, the Light of the world.
Christ, the ev - er - last - ing Lord, Je-sus, the Light of the world.
Hail the sun of righteousness, Je-sus, the Light of the world.

CHORUS.

We'll walk in the light, beautiful light, Come where the dew-drops of mer-cy are bright,

Shine all around us by day and by night, Je-sus, the Light of the world.

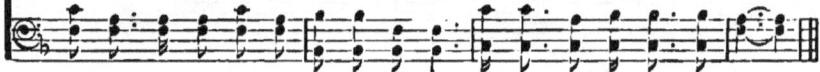

No. 88. ONWARD, CHRISTIAN SOLDIERS!

SABINE BARING-GOULD.   SULLIVAN.

1. Onward, Chris-tian sol-diers! Marching as to war, With the cross of Je-sus
2. Like a mighty army, Moves the Church of God; Brothers, we are treading
3. Crowns and thrones may perish, Kingdoms rise and wane, But the Church of Jesus
4. Onward, then, ye peo-ple, Join our happy throng, Blend with ours your voices

Go-ing on be-fore; Christ, the royal Mas-ter, Leads against the foe;
Where the saints have trod; We are not di-vid-ed, All one bod-y we,
Constant will remain: Gates of hell can never 'Gainst that Church prevail;
In the triumph-song; Glory, laud and hon-or Un-to Christ, the King,

CHORUS.

Forward in-to bat-tle, See His ban-ner go! ⎫
One in hope and doc-trine, One in char-i-ty. ⎪
We have Christ's own prom-ise, And that cannot fail. ⎬ Onward, Christian sol-diers!
This thro' countless a-ges Men and angels sing. ⎭

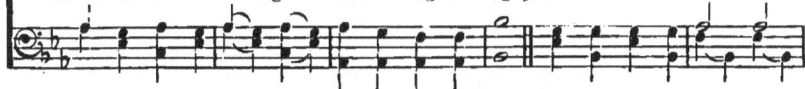

Marching as to war, With the cross of Je-sus Go-ing on be-fore.

No. 89. MARCHING TO HEAVEN.

N. A. C.

N. A. CLAPP. By per

1. We are joy-ful pilgrims, Hap-py on our way, Trav ling on the
2. We are faithful soldiers Fighting for the Lord, Gird - ed with His
3. We are hap-py Christians Singing on our way. Working in God s

road that Leads to end-less day; Walk-ing in the path where
ar - mor, Trust-ing in His word; Fight-ing in the field where
vine - yard, Toil-ing day by day; Lead ing in the path where

Angels' feet have trod, Marching on to heav-en To heav-en a-bove.
Angels feet have trod, Marching on to heav en, To heav-en a - bove.
Angels feet have trod, Oth-ers on to heav en, To heav-en a - bove.

CHORUS.

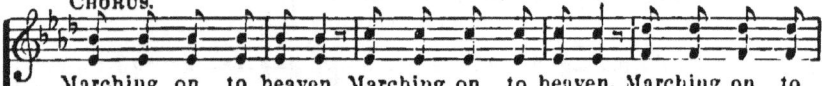

Marching on to heaven, Marching on to heaven, Marching on to

heav en, To heav - en a - bove; Lift-ing high our ban ner The

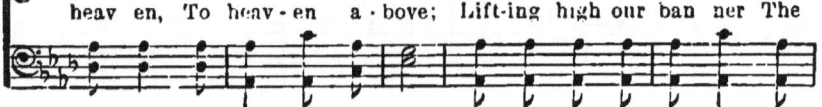

Marching to Heaven.

ban - ner of the Lord, Marching on to heav-en, To heav-en a-bove.

No. 90. **OPENING HYMN.** J. E. HALL. By per.

1. We have come to seek a bless-ing In our Father's house to-day;
2. Joy - ful - ly our songs as - cend-ing To the ev - er bless-ed One,
3. At the bell's sweet chime we gather In the house of praise and pray'r,

All His wondrous love con-fess-ing, At the throne of grace we pray;
With the an - gel notes are blending, As they chant around the throne.
Children of one lov - ing Fa - ther, Guarded by His ten - der care;

For His guidance we im-plore Him, For the wis-dom from a - bove.
Glad - ly to the o - pen por - tal, All our off'rings now we bring;
May we sing the pre-cious sto - ry Of a Sav-ior's wondrous love,

And with grateful hearts a - dore Him, For His good-ness and His love.
Heirs are we to life im - mor - tal, Sub-jects of a heav'n-ly King.
With the ransom'd saints in glo - ry, In our Fa-ther's house a - bove.

No. 91.   JESUS IS NEAR.

(Tune, "Robin Adair.")

Mrs. JENNIE KLINE.   Arr.

1. Oh, ye of lit - tle faith, What do ye fear?
2. Je - sus, our help and stay, If we en - dure:
3. This life will soon be past; End-ed its pain;

E'en in the tempest's wrath, Je-sus is near. What tho' the winds may roar?
Tri - als be - set our way, Yet we're se - cure. On Him in faith re - ly,
In peace and joy at last, Heav'n we shall gain, And with the good and pure,

What tho' the rains may pour? He is for - ev - er-more Read-y to hear.
Peace com-eth by and by; Sa-tan we can de - fy, Our rest is sure.
Dwell there for-ev - er-more, Sing with the angel choir, "Here Jesus reigns!"

No. 92.

CHO.—Jesus hears His crying children,
Gives them blessed words of cheer;
Saves them in the time of trouble;
Trust in Him without a fear.

1 When thou passest thro' the waters,
Rough and raging though they be,
Trust in Jesus, fear no evil,
In His hand He holds the sea.

2 When the storms of life are heavy,
High with waves our path is laid,
May we hear those words so cheering,
"It is I, be not afraid."

T. M. T.

No. 93. **AS FLOWS THE RIVER.**

Rev. E. Corwin   Wm. S. Pitts. By per.

Not too fast.

1. As flows the riv - er, calm and deep, In silence tow'rd the sea,
2. He kind - ly keep-eth those He loves Se - cure from ev - 'ry fear,
3. What peace He bringeth to my heart, Deep as the soundless sea!
4. How calm at e - ven sinks the sun Be-yond the cloud-ed west;

So flow-eth ev - er, and ceas-eth nev-er, The love of God for me.
From the eye that weepeth for one that sleepeth, He gen-tly dries the tear.
How sweet-ly sing-eth the soul that clingeth, My loving Lord, to Thee.
So, tem - pest-driv-en in - to the ha-ven, I reach the longed-for rest.

CHORUS.

As flows the river, calm and deep,   In silence tow'rd the sea (the sea),
                    calm and deep,

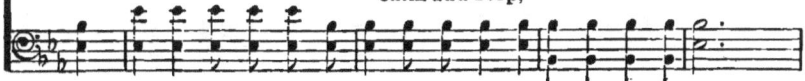

So flow-eth ev - er, and ceaseth never, The love of God to me (to me).

No. 94. WONDROUS LOVE.

DAVID C. COOK.   T. MARTIN TOWNE.

1. O wondrous love, the Fa-ther's love, Sur-pass-ing all I see,
2. It gave Him to me, as my life, My light, the truth, the way,
3. And now while worlds are rolling on, And time is pass-ing by,
4. With happy host of angel band, With lov'd ones gone above,

It gave me Je - sus for my own, It gave the Christ to me.
To heal life's troub-les, pain and strife, To lead   to end - less day.
With Je - sus ev - er by my side, I'll jour - ney to the sky.
I'll praise Him in the heav'n-ly home, I'll sing His won-drous love.

CHORUS.

Yes, won-drous love, the Fa-ther's love, The great - est love of all;

It gave me Je - sus for my own, It gave the Christ to me.

No. 95. NOTHING APART FROM THEE.

JAMES GEORGE DECK.　　(Old Air, "Juanita.")　　Arr. by T. M. T.

1. Je - sus, Thy name I love, All other names above, Je - sus, my Lord!
2. When un-to Thee I flee, Thou wilt my refuge be, Je - sus, my Lord!
3. Surely Thou'lt come again, I shall be hap-py then, Je - sus, my Lord'

Je-sus, my Lord! Oh, Thou art all to me, Noth-ing to please I see,
Je-sus, my Lord! What need I now to fear What earthly grief or care,
Je-sus, my Lord! Then Thine own face I'll see, Then I shall like Thee be,

CHORUS.

Nothing a-part from Thee, Je - sus, my Lord.)
Since Thou art ev - er near, Je - sus, my Lord. } Je - sus, my Lord,
Then ev- er-more with Thee, Je - sus, my Lord.)

Noth-ing a-part from Thee, Je - sus, my Lord, Je - sus, my Lord.

No. 96. BEAUTIFUL FACES.

T. MARTIN TOWNE.

1. Beau-ti-ful fac - es are those that wear, It mat - ters lit - tle, if
2. Beau-ti-ful lips are those whose words Leap from the heart like
3. Beau-ti-ful feet are those that go On His kind min-is - try

dark or fair, Whole-souled hon-est - y print - ed there,
songs of birds, Yet whose ut - ter - ance pru - dence girds,
to and fro, Down low-liest ways if God wills it so,

hon-est-y print - ed there. Beau-ti-ful eyes are those that show Like
ut-ter-ance pru-dence girds. Beau-ti-ful hands are those that do
if God wills it so. Beau-ti-ful shoulders are those that bear

crys - tal panes where the hearth-fires glow, Beau - ti - ful thoughts that
Work that's earnest and brave and true, Mo-ment by mo-ment the
Cease - less bur-dens of home - ly care, With pa-tient grace and

Beautiful Faces.

burn be - low, thoughts that burn be - low.
long day thro', the long   day   thro'. } Beau-ti - ful lives are
dai - ly pray'r, with grace and dai - ly pray'r.

those that bless, Sweet, si - lent riv - ers of hap - pi - uess, Whose

bidden fountains but few may guess, Whose fountains but few may guess.

Beau - ti - ful, beau - ti - ful lives, Beau - ti - ful, beau - ti - ful lives.

HE SHALL GUIDE ME.

DAVID C. COOK.   T. MARTIN TOWNE.

No. 97.

1. Be the present dark or bright, Be the fu-ture as it may,
2. Best it is to have Him Guide, Knowing He cannot do wrong:
3. Tho'ts that come from Him are pure, Words He gives are ev-er right;

God's own hand is guid-ing all, He is guid-ing all the way.
In His wis-dom and His love, He shall guide me all a-long.
Works He does thro' me en-dure, God is wis-dom, God is light.

CHORUS.

He is guiding, He is guiding, He is guid-ing all the way;

'Tis the hand that guides the world, That shall guide me all the way.

No. 98. I'VE FOUND A FRIEND.

T. MARTIN TOWNE.

1. I've found a Friend, oh, such a Friend! He loved me ere I knew Him; He
2. I've found a Friend, oh, such a Friend! All power to Him is giv-en, To
3. I've found a Friend, oh, such a Friend! So kind, and true, and ten-der, So

drew me with the cords of love, And thus He bound me to Him. And
guard me on my onward course, And bring me safe to heav-en. E-
wise a Coun-sel-or and Guide, So might-y a De-fend-er! From

'round my heart still closely twine Those ties which naught can sever, For
ter-nal glo-ries gleam a-far, To nerve my faint en-deav-or; For
Him who loves me, oh, so well, What power my heart can sev-er? For

I am His, and He is mine, For-ev-er and for-ev-er.

REFRAIN.

For I am His and He, is mine, For-ev-er and for-ev-er.

I AM LONGING TO BE FREE.

No. 99.

D. C. C.

DAVID C. COOK.
Harmonized by T. M. T.

1. I am longing, precious Je - sus, For communion sweet with Thee;
2. I have tasted of the sweetness Of Thy presence in my heart:
3. Oh, I know that there is freedom Far away from earthly care;

I am long-ing for that un - ion, For that per-fect lib - er - ty;
And I want Thee with me ev - er, With Thee no more to part;
When with Thee it's al-ways sunshine, When with Thee it's always fair;

CHORUS

I am long-ing, I am long-ing to be free. Oh, I'm

long-ing to be free, Yes, I'm long-ing to be free, I am

long-ing, pre-cious Je - sus, for Thee, pre-cious Je - sus, for Thee.

GRAND OLD DANIEL.

BELLE KELLOGG TOWNE.   T. MARTIN TOWNE. By per.

1. All a-long the Christian's pathway Snares are laid with ut-most care:
2. When temptations gath-er fierce-ly, Dark-ly hedg-ing in the way,
3. Years are passing, tears are falling, Hearts are breaking with their load:

Heed them not, but live be - liev-ing God will ev - er an-swer pray'r.
Hold on firm - ly, brave-ly, bold-ly; Morning, noon and ev'ning pray.
Lift the light of faith still high-er, Let it stream a - long the road.

CHORUS.

Let your faith, like grand old Daniel's, Brightly shine a - long the way,

Show-ing to the world a-round you, *God is with you day by day.*

No. 101. SINGING FROM THE HEART.

R. MORRIS, L. L. D.

H. R. PALMER.

MET. ♩ = 100.

1. If you have a pleasant tho't, Sing it, sing it; As the birds sing
2. Ev-'ry gracious deed of His, Sing it, sing it; Noth-ing sounds so
3. Are you weary, are you sad— Sing it, sing it; Make yourselves and

in their sport, Sing it from the heart: Does the Ho - ly Spir-it move,
well as this, Sing it from the heart; How the Lord walked on the wave,
oth - ers glad, Sing it from the heart; Bless-ed ones be - fore His face.

For the chil-dren of His love— Sing, and point the home a - bove,
Res-cued Laz-'rus from the grave, Died our guilt - y souls to save,
Sing of Christ's a - ton - ing grace, Give the Sav - ior end - less praise.

CHORUS.

Sing it from the heart. Singing, singing from the heart, Oh, the joy our

songs impart! Je - sus, bless the tune-ful art, Sing-ing from the heart.

No. 102. ALL I WANT IS THEE.

DAVID C. COOK.   T. MARTIN TOWNE.

May be sung as a Duet.

1. What, oh, what have I beside Thee, What of earth from me doth hide Thee?
2. 'Tis for Thee my heart is burning, 'Tis for Thee my soul is yearning,
3. Thou art might-y to de-liv-er, Thou, of ev-'ry good the giv-er,

All my heart goes out to find Thee, All for Thee I leave be-hind me,
On my sight Thy love is breaking, 'Tis for Thee my heart is ach-ing,
Thou canst loose the chains that bind me, Joy and peace it is to find Thee,

CHORUS.

All I want is Thee. I have felt Thy loving presence, I have known Thy

wondrous pow'r, And I long to leave sin's burdens, To be with Thee ev'ry hour.

GOD SHALL WIPE ALL TEARS AWAY.

No. 103.

D. C. C.

DAVID C. COOK.

Harmonized by T. M. T.

1. Is there sad-ness in your gladness? Soon shall come the per-fect day;
2. Is life full of care and worry? Let the heart be light and gay,
3. Casting all your care upon Him, Peace shall come the heart to stay,

He is lead-ing on to heav - en, God shall wipe all tears a - way.
He is lead-ing on to heav - en, God shall wipe all tears a - way.
He is lead-ing on to heav - en, God shall wipe all tears a - way.

CHORUS.

God shall wipe all tears a - way, God shall wipe all tears a - way,

He is lead-ing on to heav-en, God shall wipe all tears a - way.

No. 104.   AS THY DAY.

(Old Tune, "Blue Bells of Scotland.")

JULIA H. JOHNSTON.   Arr. by T. M. T.

1. Re - joice in the Lord, when the sky a - bove is bright,
2. Fear not, trembling one, for it is your Sav - ior's will
3. Oh, take from His hand all His gifts of grace and love;

Oh, trust in the dark, and "The Lord shall be thy light;"
To guide safe - ly home all who love and trust Him s'ill.
He wait - eth to bless, He is watch-ing from a - bove;

In peace, in peace a - bide, for His word is pledged to
Oh, trust Him for this day, with a heart both light and
With mer - cy ev - er new will He guide and com - fort

thee, That whate'er may be - tide, "As thy day, thy strength shall be."
free, For the Sav - ior doth say, "As thy day, thy strength shall be."
thee, For His prom-ise is true, "As thy day, thy strength shall be."

ALL IS WELL

DAVID C. COOK.　　　　　　　　T. MARTIN TOWNE.

No. 105.

1. All is well, my soul is sing-ing; All is
2. All is well by Him di - rect-ed; All the
3. All is well in pain or pleas-ure, Je - sus'
4. All is well by Him be - friend-ed, All my

well His prais-es ring-ing; All my heart its trib-ute bringing, All is
way by Him pro-tect-ed; Nev - er an - y need neg-lect-ed, All is
love no words can measure, Je - sus is my heart's best treasure, All is
life with Him at-tend-ed, All is well when life is end-ed, All is

CHORUS.

well, all is well. All is well, for He knows best, All is

well, in Him I rest: All is well, all is well, all is well.

No. 106. MAY JESUS BE WITH YOU.

D. C. C.

DAVID C. COOK.
Har. by T. M. T.

1. May Je-sus be with you, Till we meet once more, Ev-er walk be-
2. May Je-sus be with you, Till we meet once more, May the way grow
3. May Je-sus be with you, Till we meet once more, In green pastures

side you, With his grace provide you, Till we meet once more.
bright-er, Cares and burdens light-er, Till we meet once more.
lead you, Heav'nly manna feed you, Till we meet once more.

CHORUS.

May Je - sus be with you, May Je - sus be with you;

May Je - sus be with you, Till we meet in the home a - bove

No. 107.   SINGING FOR JESUS.

PHILIP PHILLIPS.

1. Sing-ing for Je - sus, sing-ing for Je - sus, Try-ing to
2. Sing-ing for Je - sus hymns of de - vo - tion, Lift-ing the
3. Sing-ing for Je - sus, bless - ed Re - deem - er, God of the

serve Him wher-ev - er I go; Pointing the lost to the way of sal-
soul on her pin-ions of love; Dropping a word or a thought by the
pil - grims, for Thee I will sing; When o'er the bil-lows of time I am

va - tion—This be my mis-sion, a pil-grim be - low, When in the
way - side, Tell-ing of rest in the mansions a - bove. Mu - sic may
waft - ed, Still with Thy praise shall e - ter - ni - ty ring. Glo-ry to

strains of my country I min-gle, When to ex - alt her my voice I would
soft-en where language would fail us, Feelings long buried 'twill often re -
God for the prospect be-fore me, Soon shall my spir - it transported as-

BY PERMISSION OF PHILIP PHILLIPS, OWNER OF COPYRIGHT.

Singing for Jesus.

raise; 'Tis for His glo - ry whose arm is her ref - uge, Him would I
store, Tones that were breathed from the lips of de - part - ed, How we re-
cend; Singing for Je - sus, Oh, bliss-ful em-ploy-ment, Loud hal-le-

hon - or, His name would I praise, His name would I praise.
vere them when they are no more, when they are no more?
lu - jahs that nev - er will end, that nev - er will end.

No. 108. Our Friend.

1 One there is above all others
   Well deserves the name of friend,
   His a love beyond a mother's,
   Costly, free, and knows no end.

Cho.—It is Jesus, it is Jesus
   It is Jesus, blessed Friend:
   Let us love Him, let us praise Him,
   Let us keep Him to the end.

2 One there is whose arm is mighty,
   One who ever will defend,
   One whose care is always o'er us,
   One who loves us to the end.

3 One there is who knows our trouble,
   One whose wisdom plans our way,
   One who loves to lead and guide us,
   One who leads to endless day.

No. 109. In the Cross.

1 In the cross of Christ I glory,
   Towering o'er the wrecks of time;
   All the light of sacred story,
   Gathers 'round its head sublime.

2 When the woes of life o'ertake me,
   Hopes deceive and fears annoy,
   Never shall the cross forsake me;
   Lo! it glows with peace and joy.

3 When the sun of bliss is beaming,
   Light and love upon my way
   From the cross the radiance streaming,
   Adds new luster to the day.

4 Bane and blessing, pain and pleasure,
   By the cross are sanctified;
   Peace is there that knows no measure,
   Joys that through all time abide.

IN THE HEAVENLY LAND.
No. 110.

D. H. L.

D. HAYDEN LLOYD. By per.

1. Oh, that land, the gold-en land, Just be-
2. In His word I read the sto - ry Of His
3. With the dear ones gone be - fore, We shall

yond the Jor-dan's strand, Where the promis'd mansions are, And the
love and dy - ing glo-ry, How on earth He came to save us, And a -
stand for-ev - er-more; There we'll watch and wait with Jesus, While the

bright and morning Star, In the heav'n-ly land be-yond, In the
bove He'll sure-ly meet us, In the bless - ed heav'nly land, In the
dear ones come and greet us, In the hap - py land be-yond, In the

CHORUS.

heav'n-ly land be-yond. In the land, far be-yond,
bless - ed heav'n-ly land.
hap - py land be-yond. Hap-py land, far beyond,

In the Heavenly Land.

In the land, bless-ed land, In the land,
heav'n-ly land, bless-ed land, heav'nly land,

far be - yond, In the heav'n - ly land be - yond.
far be-yond,

No. III. COME, YE THAT LOVE THE LORD.

Isaac Watts.   Arranged.

1. Come, ye that love the Lord, And let your joys be known;
2. Let those re - fuse to sing, Who nev - er knew our God;
3. There we shall see His face, And nev - er, nev - er sin;
4. Then let our songs a - bound, And ev - 'ry tear be dry;

Join in a song with sweet ac-cord, While ye sur-round the throne.
But chil-dren of the heav'n-ly King May speak their joys a - broad.
There, from the riv - ers of His grace, Drink endless pleasures in.
We're marching thro' Im-man-uel's ground To fair - er worlds on high.

Keep Me With Thee.

No. 112.

D. C. C.

DAVID C. COOK.
Harmonized by T. M. T.

1. Keep me with Thee, O Lord, Keep me with Thee; Drawing from Thee my life,
2. Bear - ing the fruits of love, Keep me with Thee: Gen-tle each word I speak,
3. Thro' me Thy life flow on, Keep me with Thee; Right be my ev - 'ry tho't,

Free from earth's bit-ter strife, Living with Thee, Lord, Living with Thee.
Pure ev - 'ry joy I seek, Lov-ing Thee ev - er, Liv-ing with Thee.
Lov - ing, each deed thus wrought, Flow-ing from Thee, Lord, Flowing from Thee.

CHORUS.

Keep me with Thee, Lord, Keep me with Thee: In Thee a - bid - ing,

Ev - er pro - vid-ing, Thou art un - fail-ing, Keep me with Thee.

No. 113. ALL FOR THEE.

HAVERGAL, Arr.   T. MARTIN TOWNE.

1. Take my life and let it be   Ev - er, on - ly, all for Thee;
2. Take my lips and let them be   Fill'd with mes - sag - es from Thee;
3. Take my hands and let them move At the im - pulse of Thy love;

Take my heart, it is thine own, It shall be Thy roy - al throne.
Take my voice and let me sing   Al - ways, on - ly, for my King.
Take my feet and let them be   Swift and beau - ti - ful for Thee.

CHORUS.

All for Thee, all for Thee, Precious Je - sus, all for Thee;

Take my-self, and I shall be   Ev - er, on - ly, all for Thee.

4. Take my intellect and use
   Every pow'r as Thou shalt choose;
   Take my love, my Lord, I pour
   At Thy feet its treasure-store.

5. Take my will and make it thine,
   It shall be no longer mine;
   Take my moments and my days,
   Let them flow in endless praise.

No. 114. LIGHT BEYOND.

Rev. E. A. Hoffman. J Garrison. By per.

1. Oh, how oft the feet grow weary, And how oft-en we de-spond;
2. When the brightest hopes are cherished, And our ex-pect-a-tions fond,
3. When the grave receives our lov'd ones, Sev'ring sweet af-fec-tion's bond,
4. When the darkness overspreads thee, And no joy on earth is found,

How sometimes the life grows dreary, As we sigh for joys be-yond.
Prove to be but bro-ken cisterns, Trust in God, there's light beyond.
Look to heav-en, there is sunshine, Trust in God, there's light beyond.
Up-ward turn thy wea-ry spir-it, Trust in God, there's light beyond.

CHORUS.

Trembling soul, thy Father loves thee, Why despond, oh, why de-spond?

Tho' the clouds be dark above thee, Trust in Him, there's light be-yond.

No. 115. SAVIOR, MAKE ME MORE LIKE THEE.

Rev. J. R. Atchinson.   W. S. Marshall. By per.

1. Sav-ior, make me more like Thee, This my constant pray'r shall be:
2. Sav-ior, make me more like Thee, This my song and this my plea:
3. Sav-ior, I would ev-er be Dai - ly grow-ing more like Thee:

More like Thee in heart and mind, More sub-mis-sive, more re-signed.
More like Thee in word and deed, More like Thee to those who need.
Low - ly, gen - tle, pa-tient, meek, All Thy grac - es, Lord, I seek.

More like Thee in dai - ly life, Free from an - ger, free from strife:
Full of sym - pa - thy and love; Give me wis - dom from a - bove:
All Thy mind to me im - part, Wash my hands, my head, my heart;

That I may be more like Thee, Sav - ior, come a - bide with me.
That I may be more like Thee, Draw me clos - er, Lord, to Thee.
Thou didst come to be like me, By and by I'll be like Thee.

No. 116.
JESUS HAS ENTERED MY SOUL.

DAVID C. COOK.   T. MARTIN TOWNE.

1. My heart it is bright with a heav-en - ly light, For
2. The treasure of heav'n unto me has been giv'n, For
3. No love can compare with the love that is there, For

Je - sus has en-tered my soul; The darkness and night have taken their flight,
Je - sus has en-tered my soul; My heart has a joy which naught can destroy,
Je - sus has en-tered my soul; No ill can be-tide, no sor-row a - bide,

CHORUS.

For Je - sus has en-tered my soul. Yes, Je - sus has en-tered my

soul, Je - sus has en-tered my soul: And my heart it is bright

with a heav-en - ly light, For Je-sus has en-tered my soul.

No. 117. HIS EVERLASTING ARMS.

D. C. C.

David C. Cook.
Harmonized by T. M. T.

1. Oh, "He shall preserve my go - ing;" "Un - der-neath me are His
2. His strength shall support the hum-ble, "Un - der-neath me are His
3. No, noth-ing from Him can sev - er; "Un - der-neath me are His

ev - er - last-ing arms;" Where the liv - ing wa - ters are flow-ing,
ev - er - last-ing arms:" I shall nev - er fal - ter nor stum-ble,
ev - er - last-ing arms;" In His arms He shall bear me ev - er,

CHORUS.

He shall bear me on. Then I'll nev - er stumble on the jour - ney,

Then I'll nev - er fal - ter on the way: In the shad - ow or

in the sun - light, In the dark - ness or in the day.

IN THE ARK OF HIS LOVE.

No. 118.

NETTIE J. HUNT.

T. MARTIN TOWNE.

From "Lost and Saved," by per.

1. There's a place for the Christian to hide In the hour of his
2. It is far from the world's noisy strife, Far away from the
3. O toil - ers by sor-row oppressed, Come en-ter this

sor-row and woe; When beateth dark grief's angry tide, Oh, 'tis
tur-moil of sin. None know of its "new-ness of life," Save
joy - ful a - bode, Come, taste of its sweetness and rest, And

sweet of that ref - uge to know.
those who in joy en - ter in. } In the ark of His love, of His
cast off your sin - giv - en load.

CHORUS.

love,.......... In the se - cret pa - vil - ion of God;.......
love, of His love, of God;

In the Ark of His Love.

In the ark of His love, of His love, In the secret pa-vil-ion of God.

No. 119.

Mrs. M. E. Cox.

LEAN ON JESUS.

J. C. Macy. By per.

With animation.

1. If a sor-row, dark and heav-y, Casts its shad-ow o'er your way,
2. What tho' in your youth's fair morning, Noblest work you planned to do,
3. If, in-stead of high-est pathways, Low-ly ones on earth you tread,
4. Aft-er earn-est, strong en-deav-or, Pa-tient toil for ma-ny years,
5. It will spring and bear rich harvest; Good seed is not sown in vain;

FINE.

Blot-ting out hope's bless-ed sun-light, And you have no words to pray,
Strangely all your plans were thwarted, How or why you nev-er knew.
Do not deem your life a fail-ure, Nor let use-less tears be shed.
Hearts grow weary, and your la-bor Al-most with-out fruit ap-pears,
Pres-ent chast'ning seemeth grievous, Yet will prove e-ter-nal gain.

D.S. *Blest as-sur-ance He has giv-en, Night shall end in per-fect day.*

CHORUS.

D. S.

Lean on Je-sus, lean on Je-sus, Tho' you can-not see the way;

No. 120. JESUS SAVES FROM SIN.

David C. Cook.   T. Martin Towne.

Earnestly.

1. Out of sin's sad bondage, Je-sus bids us come,   Jesus saves from sin,
2. Tell the joyous ti-dings o-ver land and sea,   Jesus saves from sin,
3. No more care and bondage, no more Satan's reign, Jesus saves from sin,
4. Je-sus, constant Savior, keep us close to Thee, Jesus saves from sin.

Je - sus saves from sin.   Un - to joy and free-dom,   un - to
Je - sus saves from sin.   Je - sus' pow'r is might-y,   Je - sus
Je - sus saves from sin.   Ev - er rest and free-dom,   Sa - tan's
Je - sus saves from sin.   Sin no more is mas-ter,   Je - sus

heav'n our home, Je - sus saves from sin,   Je-sus saves from sin.
sav-eth me,   Je - sus saves from sin,   Je-sus saves from sin.
pow'r is vain,   Je - sus saves from sin,   Je-sus saves from sin.
keeps us free,   Je - sus saves from sin,   Je-sus saves from sin.

CHORUS.

Je-sus saves from sin, Jesus saves from sin: From its bondage frees us,

Jesus Saves from Sin.

From its pois-on heals us, Jesus saves from sin, Je-sus saves from sin.

No. 121.

1 Jesus. lover of my soul.
  Let me to Thy bosom fly,
While the waters near me roll.
  While the tempest still is high:
Hide me. O my Savior. hide,
  Till the storm of life is past:
Safe into the haven guide,
  Oh, receive my soul at last.

2 Other refuge have I none:
  Hangs my helpless soul on Thee:
Leave, oh. leave me not alone:
  Still support and comfort me:
All my trust on Thee is stayed:
  All my help from Thee I bring:
Cover my defenseless head
  With the shadow of Thy wing.

3 Thou, O Christ, art all I want:
  More than all in Thee I find:
Raise the fallen, cheer the faint,
  Heal the sick, and lead the blind:
Just and holy is Thy name:
  I am all unrighteousness:
False, and full of sin I am;
  Thou art full of truth and grace.

4 Plenteous grace with Thee is found,
  Grace to cover all my sin:
Let the healing streams abound:
  Make and keep me pure within.
Thou of life the fountain art;
  Freely let me take of Thee:
Spring Thou up within my heart;
  Rise to all eternity.

No. 122.

1 My Jesus, I love Thee,
  I know Thou art mine,
For Thee all the follies
  Of sin I resign;
My gracious Redeemer,
  My Savior art Thou,
If ever I loved Thee,
  My Jesus, 'tis now.

2 I love Thee, because Thou
  Hast first loved me,
And purchased my pardon
  On Calvary's tree:
I love Thee for wearing
  The thorns on Thy brow;
If ever I loved Thee,
  My Jesus, 'tis now.

3 I will love Thee in life,
  I will love Thee in death.
And praise Thee as long as
  Thou lendest me breath;
And say when the death-dew
  Lies cold on my brow,
If ever I loved Thee,
  My Jesus, 'tis now.

4 In mansions of glory
  And endless delight,
I'll ever adore Thee
  In heaven so bright:
I'll sing with the glittering
  Crown on my brow,
If ever I loved Thee,
  My Jesus, 'tis now.
         London Hymn Book.

No. 123. WE ARE COMING TO THE LIGHT.

D. C. C.

DAVID C. COOK.
Har. by T M. T.

1. We are com-ing to the light, For we want to know the right,
2. Oh, our hearts are all   for thee, And our lives would ev - er be,
3. Oh, that all the world might see, The blest light and life in Thee,

And   be free from sin and darkness, So we're coming to the light.
In   the light for - ev - er glow-ing, So we're coming to the light.
Make our lives for - ev - er bea-cons Light-ing oth-ers   to thy-self.

CHORUS.

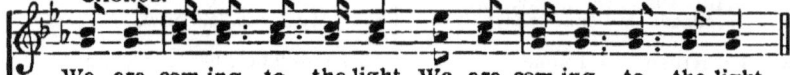

We are com-ing to the light, We are com-ing to the light,

We are com-ing bless-ed Je - sus, to Thee, 'Tis the

light, the life of men, 'Tis re-newed on earth a - gain In the

We are Coming to the Light.

hearts of those who love Thee, And we're com-ing to the light.

No. 124. In Heav'nly Love.

1 In heavenly love abiding,
No change my heart shall fear:
And safe is such confiding,
For nothing changes here.
The storm may roar without me,
My heart may low be laid,
But God is 'round about me,
And can I be dismayed?

2 Wherever He may guide me,
No want shall turn me back,
My Shepherd is beside me,
And nothing can I lack.
His wisdom ever waketh,
His sight is never dim,
He knows the way He taketh,
And I will walk with Him.

3 Green pastures are before me,
Which yet I have not seen;
Bright skies will soon be o'er me,
Where darkest clouds have been.
My hope I cannot measure,
My path to life is free,
My Savior has my treasure,
And He will walk with me.
ANNA L. WARING.

No.125. All Hail the Power.

1 All hail the power of Jesus' name!
Let angels prostrate fall;
Bring forth the royal diadem,
And crown Him Lord of all

2 Ye chosen seed of Israel's race,
Ye ransomed from the fall,
Hail Him who saves you by His grace,
And crown Him Lord of all.

3 Sinners, whose love can ne'er forget
The wormwood and the gall,
Go, spread your trophies at His feet,
And crown Him Lord of all.

4 Let every kindred, every tribe,
On this terrestrial ball,
To Him all majesty ascribe,
And crown Him Lord of all.
REV. EDWARD PERRONET.

No. 126. Holy Spirit.

1 Holy Spirit, faithful Guide,
Ever near the Christian's side,
Gently lead us by the hand,
Pilgrims in a desert land.
Weary souls fore'er rejoice,
While they hear that sweetest voice
Whispering softly, "Wanderer, come,
Follow me, I'll guide thee home."

2 Ever present, truest Friend,
Ever near, Thine aid to lend;
Leave us not to doubt and fear,
Groping on in darkness drear.
When the storms are raging sore,
Hearts grow faint,and hopes give o'er,
Whisper softly, "Wanderer, come,
Follow me, I'll guide thee home."

HARK! THE VOICE OF JESUS.

Rev. Daniel March.   Rev. Morrison. By per.

No. 127.

1. Hark! the voice of Je-sus calling, "Who will go and work to-day?
2. If you can-not cross the ocean, And the heathen land explore,
3. If you can-not speak like angels, If you cannot preach like Paul,
4. While the souls of men are dying, And the Master calls for you.

Fields are white, the har-vest wait-ing, Who will bear the sheaves a - way?
You can find the hea-then near-er, You can help them at the door.
You can tell the love of Je-sus, You can say He died for all.
Let none hear you i - dly say-ing, "There is noth-ing I can do."

Loud and long the Mas - ter call-eth, Rich re-ward He of - fers thee:
If you cannot give your thousands, You can give your widow's mite;
If you fail to rouse the wick-ed With the judgment's dread a-larms,
Glad - ly take the task He gives you, Let His work your pleasure be:

Who will an-swer. glad - ly say-ing, "Here am I, O Lord, send me."
And the least you do for Je - sus, Will be pre-cious in His sight.
You may lead the lit - tle chil-dren To the Sav-ior's lov - ing arms.
An - swer quickly when He call-eth, "Here am I, O Lord, send me."

No. 128.   PERFECT IN THEE.

Old Air, "Oft in the Stilly Night."

DAVID C. COOK.   Arranged by T. M. T.

1. A - lone thro' Thee is vic - to - ry, Thou art my joy and crown;
2. My soul a - way to realms of day, Would high-er take its flight;
3. It is Thy will, Thy bless-ed will, That I should per - fect be;

A-lone to Thee, the glo - ry be, To Thee be all re - nown.
On Thee re - ly, still up - ward fly, Thy love shall bear me right.
Thy love un - told, shall me up - hold, My life be lost in Thee.

CHORUS.

To Thee, to Thee, the glo - ry be, To Thee, my Sav - ior dear,

My soul goes sing - ing all the way, For Thou art all to me.

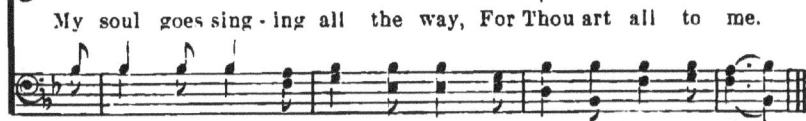

No. 129.   FIRST FOR JESUS.

D. C. C.

DAVID C COOK.
Harmonized by T. M. T.

1. First tho'ts for Je-sus, Best tho'ts for Thee; So to be good and true,
2. First work for Je-sus, Best work for Thee; So may my work be right,
3. First tho'ts of Je-sus, Best tho'ts of Thee; So may I al-ways be
4. First love for Je-sus, Best love for Thee; Touched by Thy lov-ing smile,
5. First, ALL for Je-sus, First, ALL for Thee; So may my treasure be

Right be in all I do, Right in the great and small, Act right by all.
Ev - er as in Thy sight Work that shall stand the test, Work all the best.
Clos-est of all to Thee, Hap-py my life shall be, Al-ways with Thee.
Be lov-ing all the while, Lov-ing to great and small, Lov-ing to all.
Such as is good to Thee, Treasure that shall endure, All that is pure.

CHORUS.

Let Je-sus be first, first, Let Je-sus be first;

Let Je-sus be first in ev'rything with you, None cares so much for thee,

First for Jesus.

None loves so ten-der-ly, None is so wise as He, Let Je - sus be first.

No. 130.

1 To-day the Savior calls;
Ye wanderers, come;
O ye benighted souls,
Why longer roam?

2 To-day the Savior calls;
Oh, listen now!
Within these sacred walls
To Jesus bow.

3 The Spirit calls to-day;
Yield to His power;
Oh, grieve Him not away;
'Tis mercy's hour.
S. F. SMITH, D. D.

No. 131.

1 What though the load be heavy
What though the road be steep.
What though my feet grow weary.
Christ my soul will keep.
If what He asks seems grievous,
Yet will I quick obey,
For I am sure He loves me,
And will find a way.

2 What though the hand grow weary,
What though the eye grow dim;
Jesus has bid me trust Him,
Cast my care on Him;
So, in the dark or sunshine,
Close by my Savior's side,
Yielding my hand to Jesus,
Trust Him as my guide.
Rev. L. F. COLE.

No. 132.

1 More love to Thee, O Christ!
More love to Thee;
Hear Thou the prayer I make
On bended knee:
This is my earnest plea,
More love, O Christ, to Thee,
More love to Thee!
More love to Thee!

2 Once earthly joy I craved,
Sought peace and rest:
Now Thee alone I seek,
Give what is best:
This all my prayer shall be,
More love, O Christ, to Thee,
More love to Thee!
More love to Thee!

3 Let sorrow do its work,
Send grief and pain:
Sweet are Thy messengers,
Sweet their refrain,
When they can sing with me,—
More love, O Christ, to Thee,
More love to Thee!
More love to Thee!

4 Then shall my latest breath
Whisper Thy praise;
This be the parting cry
My heart shall raise;
This still its prayer shall be:
More love, O Christ, to Thee,
More love to Thee!
More love to Thee!
MRS. ELIZABETH PRENTISS.

No. 133. THE MORNING STAR.

Rev. Rob't Kerr.   W. Irving Hartshorn. By per.

Happily.

1. How sweetly Christ, the morn-ing star, Shines on our pil · grim way,
2. When tossed on life's wide heaving sea, Where tempests wild - ly rave,
3. The beauteous star that shines on us, Fore - tells the dawn of day,

To guide us thro' the night of time To heav'n's un - cloud-ed day.
His beams bring cheer and ban-ish fear, And gild the troubled wave.
Be - fore whose face all e - vil things Shall swift-ly flee a · way.

CHORUS.

To Him we raise our grate-ful song, Whose glo-ry from a - far

Makes glad our hearts and lights our path, The bright and Morning Star

No. 134. **FOLLOWING JESUS.**

Rev. A. A. HOSKIN. W. S. PITTS. By per.

1. Fol-low-ing Je - sus day by day, Walking with Him the narrow way;
2. Fol-low-ing Je - sus. leaving all, Glad to o - bey His heav'nly call:
3. Fol-low-ing Him and growing strong, Doing the right and shunning wrong;
4. Fol-low-ing Him while life is giv'n, Following Christ to home in heav'n;

Close to His steps our feet shall cling, Following Je-sus while we sing.
Free-ly our lives to Him we bring, Following Je-sus while we sing.
Safe from the tempter, 'neath His wing, Following Je-sus while we sing.
Sweeter our prais-es there shall ring, Following Je-sus while we sing.

CHORUS.

Following, following ev-'ry day, Following Christ in the heavenly way;

Following, following all our lives long, Following Jesus with service and song.

No. 135.　REST.

D. C. C.

DAVID C. COOK.
Harmonized by T. M. T.

1. Rest! there is rest for the weary; Rest on the Savior's
2. Wea-ry and heav - y laden, Sorrow-bowed down, op-
3. Ev - er in Him I'm finding, Find-ing rest, sweet

breast; Bring Him your ev - 'ry bur-den, Rest, there is rest, sweet rest.
pressed, Oh, how His arms can rest you, Rest, there is rest, sweet rest.
rest; Ev - er His arms a - bout me, Ev - er up - on His breast.

CHORUS.

Rest, rest, rest,..... Rest on the Sav - ior's bo - som; Rest on the
rest, sweet rest,

Savior's breast; Oh, to be ev - er rest-ing; Rest, rest, sweet rest.

No. 136.   PEACE WITH GOD.

Eliza Sherman.   W. Irving Hartshorn. By per.

1. Peace with God, what gift more pre - cious; All earth's cares and trials cease,
2. Peace with God that flow-eth ev - er, As   a   riv - er, pure and deep,
3. Peace with God that passeth knowledge, On His precious word we rest,

When, like sweetest ben - e - dic-tion Comes this gift of per-fect peace.
Thro' the sunshine and the shad-ow, Thro' our wak-ing and our sleep.
Trust-ing in His lov-ing kind-ness, Ly - ing calm-ly on His breast.

CHORUS.

Peace with God! a peace so per-fect, Earthly cares from troubling cease;

When the heart is stayed upon Him, Je - sus giv-eth per-fect peace.

No. 137. OH, FOR A THOUSAND TONGUES.

Old Air, "Away the Bowl."

WESLEY.

Arr. by T. M. T.

1. Oh, for a thousand tongues to sing My great Re-deem - er's praise:
2. Je - sus! the name that charms our fears, That bids our sor - row cease;

The glo - ries of my God and King, The tri - umphs of His grace!
'Tis mu - sic in the sin - ner's ears; 'Tis life, and health, and peace.

My gra-cious Mas-ter, and my God, As - sist me to pro - claim,—
He speaks, and, list'ning to His voice,—New life the dead re - ceive;

To spread thro' all the earth a-broad, The hon - ors of Thy name.
The mournful, bro-ken hearts re-joice; The hum-ble poor be - lieve.

No. 138.   TELL ME ALL ABOUT JESUS.

Rev. Elisha A. Hoffman.   Joseph Garrison. By per.

1. Tell me all a-bout Je - sus, Who came from heav'n a - bove:
2. Tell me all a-bout Je - sus, Who dai - ly cares for me·
3. Tell me all a-bout Je - sus, Re - peat the sto - ry o'er,

Tell me more of His good - ness, More of His pre-cious love.
Tell me why He should love me, Why He should die for me.
Nev-er shall I grow wea - ry, Hear-ing it more and more.

CHORUS.

Tell me all a - bout Je - sus, Tell me that I may know,

The sto - ry of the Sav - ior, Who loves, who loves me so.

No. 139.

AWAKE! AWAKE!

E. B. HOLLIS.
J. M. STILLMAN.

Con spirito.

1. A - wak - en, ye who slum-ber, The foe is at the gates;
2. The bat - tle-cry is ring - ing Wher - ev - er sin is found;
3. This is no time for sleep-ing, Be - fore you is the foe;

A host no man can num-ber, Up - on your Cap - tain waits,
The bat - tle-song they're sing-ing, The whole wide earth a - round.
With stealthy step he's creep-ing, Spring up and lay him low;

Yet you are i - dly sleep-ing, As if with naught to do,
Up, then, and join their num - ber, Your place no one can fill;
Fling wide a - broad the ban - ner, Of Christ, your Lord and King,

While an - gel eyes are keep - ing An anx-ious watch on you.
Up from this sloth - ful slum - ber, And fight with heart and will.
And shout a loud ho - san - na, Till heav'n's high arch-es ring.

Awake! Awake!

CHORUS.

A-wake! A-wake! Your sta - tion take, And fight to win your crown;

A-wake! A-wake! Your sta - tion take, And fight to win your crown.

No. 140.

1 Sun of my soul, my Savior dear,
It is not night if Thou be near:
Oh, may no earthborn cloud arise,
To hide Thee from my waiting eyes.

2 Abide with us from morn till eve,
For without Thee we cannot live;
Abide with us when night is nigh,
For without Thee we dare not die.

3 Watch by the sick; enrich the poor
With blessings from Thy boundless
  store;
Be every mourner's sleep to-night
Like infants' slumbers, pure and light.

4 Come near and bless us when we
  wake,
Ere through the world our way we take,
Till in the ocean of Thy love
We lose ourselves in heaven above.

J. KEBLE.

No. 141.

1 My days are gliding swiftly by,
And I, a pilgrim stranger,
Would not detain them as they fly,
Those hours of toil and danger.

CHO.—For oh, we stand on Jordan's
  strand,
Our friends are passing over,
And just before, the shining shore
We may almost discover.

2 Should coming days be cold and dark,
We need not cease our singing;
That perfect rest naught can molest,
Where golden harps are ringing.

3 Let sorrow's rudest tempest blow,
Each chord on earth to sever;
Our King says Come, and there's our
  home,
Forever, oh, forever.

Rev. DAVID NELSON, 1835.

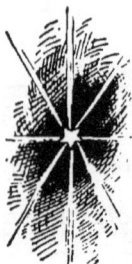

No. 142. JESUS BIDS US SHINE.

ANNA BARTLETT WARNER.   T. M. TOWNE.

1. Je-sus bids us shine with a clear. pure light, Like a lit-tle
2. Je-sus bids us shine first of all for Him; Well He sees and
3. Je-sus bids us shine, then, for all a-round; Ma - ny kinds of

can - dle,   burn-ing   in the night   In this world of dark- ness,
knows it   if our lights are dim.   He looks down from heav-en,
dark - ness   in this world are found;   Sin and want and sor - row:

we   must shine, You in your small cor - ner, and I   in mine.
to see us   shine, You in your small cor - ner, and I   in mine.
so we may shine, You in your small cor - ner, and I   in mine.

No. 143. God is Love.

1 God is love; His mercy brightens
   All the path in which we rove;
Bliss He wakes, and woe He lightens:
   God is wisdom, God is love.
Chance and change are busy ever;
   Man decays and ages move;

But His mercy waneth never;
   God is wisdom, God is love.

2 E'en the hour that darkest seemeth
   Will His changeless goodness prove;
From the mist His brightness streameth;
   God is wisdom, God is love.
He with earthly cares entwineth
   Hope and comfort from above;
Everywhere His glory shineth:
   God is wisdom, God is love.

Sir JOHN BOWRING.

No. 144.   SWEET HEAVENLAND.

Old Air, "Maryland, my Maryland."

MATTIE PEARSON SMITH.   Arranged.

1. O glorious land—by faith I see— Heav-en-land, sweet heav-en-land,
2. In thee is found no bro-ken heart, Heav-en-land, sweet heav-en-land,
3. In thee no sin my soul can sway, Heav-en-land, sweet heav-en-land,
4. O land of pur - est love and bliss, Heav-en-land, sweet heav-en-land,

A-round thee rolls the crys-tal sea, Heavenland, sweet heavenland;
And friend from friend shall never part, Heavenland, sweet heavenland;
My tears will all be wiped a - way, Heavenland, sweet heavenland;
O bless-ed place where Je - sus is, Heavenland, sweet heavenland;

No scorching winds nor searching cold, No cares nor sorrows man - i - fold:
But with the hosts in bright ar-ray, Will dwell in peace thro' endless day,
Although my days have e - vil been, Yet if redeemed from all my sin,
When I a - wake be - yond the tide, In His sweet likeness glo - ri - fied,

A hap-py place where none grows old, Heavenland, sweet heavenland.
And none from thee will ev - er stray, Heavenland, sweet heavenland.
My God will grant me entrance in Heavenland, sweet heavenland.
I know I shall be sat - is - fied, Heavenland, sweet heavenland.

No. 145.   GOD IS LOVE.

M. H. HOWLISTON.

1. Do you know what the dew-drops say, . . .   As they sparkle at
2. Do you know what the sun-beams bright. .   Are sing-ing from

CHORUS.

break of day?   It is love, love, love,   Our God is a God of
morning till night?

love.   It is love, love, love,   Our God is a God of love.

3. Do you know what the soft rain tells,
   As it tinkles like fairy bells?

4. Do you know what the winds proclaim,
   As they rustle the golden grain:

FROM THE "CHILD'S SONG-BOOK," BY PER

No. 146. HO! CHRISTIAN, BE THOU ACTIVE.

MARGARETTE W. SNODGRASS.   DR. J. B. HERBERT.

1. Ho! Chris-tian, be thou act-ive, For Christ thy Lord is near:
2. Re - ward He bring-eth with Him, And He will bring to thee,
3. Lift up thine eyes, O Chris-tian! His glo - ry streams a - far;

D.C.—*Ho! Chris-tian, be thou act - ive, For Christ thy Lord is near;*

FINE.

Thou know-est not the mo-ment In which He shall ap - pear.
Ac - cord - ing to the meas-ure Of what thy work shall be;
He shin - eth in His beau - ty, "The bright and Morn-ing Star."

Thou know - est not the mo-ment In which He shall ap - pear.

Be - hold, He com - eth quick-ly, Oh, may He come to - day,
And those He call - eth bless - ed, Who His com-mand-ment do,
Go spread His in - vi - ta-tion, Go ring it forth un - til

D.C.

To thrill you with His glad-ness, Not fill you with dis - may.
They at the gates of heav - en Shall find an en-trance through.
Thro' all the world has sound-ed, "Come, who - so - ev - er will."

No. 147. ENTER IN.

E. CORWIN, D. D.　　　　　　　　　T. MARTIN TOWNE.

1. Heav'n is worth the earn-est seek-ing, En - ter in,
2. With thee now the Sav- ior plead-eth, En - ter in,
3. Heark - en to the voic - es cry - ing, En - ter in,

en - ter in; This the word that Christ is speaking, Enter, en - ter in.
en - ter in; This the way to life that leadeth, En - ter, en - ter in.
en - ter in; Take His cross, thyself de - ny-ing, En - ter, en - ter in.

He who feeds the fall-ing spar-row, Cares to res - cue us from sin;
From the way of death de-part-ing, Leav-ing all the paths of sin,
List - en to the voice of conscience As it gen - tly speaks with-in;

En - ter, tho' the gate be nar - row, En - ter, en - ter in.
Ev - 'ry e - vil course for - sak - ing, En - ter, en - ter in.
Hast-en to the way of safe - ty, En - ter, en - ter in.

No. 148. I'LL GIVE MY HEART TO THEE.

J. C. M.

J. C. MACY. By per.

Gladly.

1. Lov-ing, I'll go to the Sav-ior's side. Bless-ed Je-sus, He will pro-vide!
2. Singing so joy-ous-ly, an-gels stand, Shin-ing host of the promised land,
3. Ten-der-ly car-ing for you and me, Je-sus giv-eth His love so free!

And He will o-pen the gates so wide, To bid me en-ter in.
Glad that I've given my heart and hand To Christ, the Lord of all.
Haste, then, His du-ti-ful child to be, And ye shall en-ter in.

CHORUS. *f*

Yes, lov-ing, I'll go to Him, All sor-rows I'll
Yes, lov-ing, etc.
Yes, lov-ing, we'll go to Him, All sor-rows we'll

Yes, I will go, go to Him, Sor-row and care

leave with Him; My heart will I give to Him, Christ, the Savior dear.
leave with Him; Glad hearts will we bring to Him, Christ, the Savior dear.

Savior dear.

leave with Him:

No. 149. WORK AND PRAY.

Kate Sumner Burr.

M. J. Munger. By per.

1. Up, friends of Je - sus, the har-vest now is white, Work will soon be
2. Up, friends of Je - sus, for time will soon be o'er, Har-vest days are
3. Shout, friends of Je-sus, for when our work is done, Joy - ful we will

o - ver, fast falls the shade of night; Strong in His strength, let us
pass-ing to come a-gain no more; Wake from re - pose, hear the
gath - er to greet the har-vest home; Then let us hast - en the

bind the golden sheaves, Could we meet the Master with naught but leaves?
Mas - ter call-ing still, Rise to earn-est ef - fort with right good will.
gold-en sheaves to bind, Rest and life e - ter - nal we all shall find.

CHORUS.

Work and pray,.......... yes, work and pray, Let the
Work and pray, work and pray,

Work and Pray.

watch-word pass a - long, Work and pray,......... Now while 'tis work and pray,

day, Come and join our hap - py throng. while 'tis day,

No. 150.

1 Awake, my soul, in joyful lays,
And sing thy great Redeemer's praise;
He justly claims a song from me,
His loving-kindness is so free.

2 Through mighty hosts of cruel foes,
Where earth and hell my way oppose,
He safely leads my soul along,
His loving-kindness is so strong.

3 So when I pass death's gloomy vale,
And life and mortal powers shall fail,
Oh, may my last expiring breath
His loving-kindness sing in death.

4 Then shall I mount and soar away
To the bright world of endless day:
There shall I sing, with sweet surprise,
His loving-kindness in the skies.

Rev. SAMUEL MEDLEY.

No. 151.

1 Ask, and it shall be given,
‾ Seek Him and you shall find,
Knock and it shall be opened,
For the Lord is kind.
Come with the faith of children,
Trusting a Savior's love,
Tell Him your wants are many;
Look in faith above.

2 Pray in the early morning,
Pray in the golden noon,
Pray in the starlight gloaming,
Faith brings answer soon.
Prayer is a precious incense,
Always to Him most dear;
His kindness faileth never,
He will surely hear.

MARIAN W. HUBBARD.

No. 152. DRAW ME TO THEE.

DAVID C. COOK.
Harmonized by T. M. T.

D. C. C.

1. What is it keeps me' from the fold? Why do I stay in the
2. Is it the tempter's cru - el hold, Have I by self un - to
3. How I have suffered be-cause of sin, How I have prayed for Thy

dark-ness and cold? Why do I suf - fer this an-guish un - told?
him been sold? Je - sus o'er Sa - tan has pow - er un - told,
com-ing with-in, How I have longed for Thy life to be - gin,

CHORUS.

O Je-sus, draw me to Thee. Je - sus, my heart is yearning for Thee,

Jesus, my heart is yearning for Thee, Come to my rescue, dear Savior, to-day,

Draw Me to Thee.

Rit.

Break ev'ry bond that keeps me a-way, O Je-sus, draw me to Thee.

No. 153.

1 Nearer, my God, to Thee,
  Nearer to Thee;
E'en though it be a cross
  That raiseth me,
Still all my song shall be,
Nearer, my God, to Thee.—*Nearer, etc.*

2 Though like a wanderer,
    Daylight all gone,
Darkness be over me,
    My rest a stone,
Yet in my dreams I'd be
Nearer, my God, to Thee.—*Nearer, etc.*

3 There let the way appear
    Steps up to heaven;
All that Thou sendest me,
    In mercy given.
Angels to beckon me
Nearer, my God, to Thee.—*Nearer, etc.*

4 Then with my waking thoughts
    Bright with Thy praise,
Out of my stony griefs.
    Bethel I'll raise;
So by my woes to be
Nearer, my God, to Thee.—*Nearer, etc.*

SARAH F. ADAMS.

No. 154.

1 Lord, I hear of showers of blessing
  Thou art scattering full and free—
Showers, the thirsty land refreshing;
  Let some droppings fall on me—

REF.—Even me, even me.
      Let Thy blessing fall on me.

2 Pass me not, O gracious Father!
    Sinful though my heart may be;
Thou might'st leave me, but the rather
    Let Thy mercy fall on me—

3 Pass me not, O tender Savior!
    Let me love and cling to Thee
I am longing for Thy favor;
    Whilst Thou'rt calling, oh, call me—

4 Pass me not! Thy lost one bringing,
    Bind my heart, O Lord, to Thee;
While the streams of life are springing,
    Blessing others, oh, bless me.

MRS. ELIZ. CODNER.

No. 155.

1 There's a wideness in God's mercy
    Like the wideness of the sea:
There's a kindness in His justice
    Which is more than liberty.

REF.—He is calling, "Come to me!'
      Lord. I gladly haste to Thee.

2 For the love of God is broader
    Than the measure of man's mind;
And the heart of the Eternal
    Is most wonderfully kind.

3 If our love were but more simple,
    We should take Him at His word;
And our lives would be all sunshine,
    In the sweetness of our Lord.

F. W. FABER.

No. 156. THE KINDEST RULE.

SUSIE M. DAY.   A. T. GORAM. By per.

1. Kind-er rule of earth-ly du - ty Wis-est men could nev - er give;
2. Are we tempt-ed to be self-ish, An-gry, harsh, un-kind, un-true?
3. We would nev - er show to oth-ers Scornful, proud, un-lov - ing face,

Sweet-er rule of heav'n-ly beau - ty Need we nev - er while we live.
Hear the voice of conscience whisper, "Would you have this done to you?"
Knowing not what our lives might be, Had God put us in their place.

What-so - ev - er deeds of kindness We may wish that men may do,
Few - er wounds would then be giv-en, Few - er bit - ter words be said;
From our hearts should first be driven All the thoughts of wrong and strife,

Un - to oth - ers we must ev - er Show these lov - ing ac-tions, too.
Few - er acts to be re - gret-ted, When the ones we love are dead.
Ere we have the right to cen-sure What we see in oth - er's life.

The Kindest Rule.

REFRAIN.

Kind-er rule of earth - ly du - ty, Sweet-er rule of heav'n - ly

beau-ty, Sweeter rule of heav'nly beauty, Need we nev - er while we live.

No. 157. HAPPY IN JESUS.

(Sing to Tune on Opposite Page.)

1 I am happy, oh, so happy.
   Precious Savior, in Thy love;
I could sing from morn till even,
   Like the blessed ones above.
I could tell of Thy sweet mercy
   Through the bright, bright, sunny day,
And in joy and adoration
   Pass the blissful hours away.

REFRAIN.—I am happy, oh, so happy,
   I am happy, oh, so happy,
   I am happy, yes, I'm happy,
   Precious Savior, in Thy love.

2 I am happy, oh, so happy.
   For I know that Thou art mine,
And Thy Spirit witness whispers
   That I am a child of Thine;
And an heir to life and glory
   In the deathless summer land,
Where with saints and shining angels
   In my white robes I shall stand.

3 I am happy, oh, so happy.
   And my heart is light and free
As the bonnie birds above me,
   Warbling joyous melody;
I will sing of Thee, my Savior,
   Bless Thee with my feeble breath,
Till my eyes are closed to life-light,
   And my earth-songs hushed in death.

A. T. GORAM.

No. 158. I AM WAITING, DEAR JESUS, FOR THEE.

J. G.

JOSEPH GARRISON. By per.

1. I am wait-ing for Je-sus to wel-come me home, To the
2. How I long to be roam-ing the blest fields of light, With the
3. Ma-ny loved ones have I in that beau-ti-ful land, They are
4. Roll along, then, sweet moments, and bear me a-way To my

place He has gone to pre-pare, To the mansion of light and the
dear, lov-ing chil-dren of light; And to sing the sweet song as we're
watching and wait-ing for me; And they beckon me o'er to that
beau-ti-ful home in the sky, To the land of the blest, where I

CHORUS.

robe, pure and white, To the harp and the crown for me there. } Wait - ing,
marching a-long, Of redemption thro' Je - sus' might. } Waiting, dear Jesus, yes,
bright happy shore, There the beauties of heaven to see. } Ev - er.
sweetly shall rest In the pal-ace of Je-sus on high. } Ever I'm longing, dear

wait - ing, I am waiting, dear Jesus, for Thee;
waiting for Thee.
long - ing, All the beauties of [Omit. . . . .] heaven to see.
Jesus, I'm longing,

No. 159.   THE SHINING CITY.

THOS. L. M. TIPTON.   E. H. BAILEY. By per.

Moderato.

1. Far, far away o'er the si-lent sea, Far off on that shining shore,
2. O cit-y of God, it is build-ed fair, On high, on the ho-ly hill;
3. Fair cit-y, it tow'reth the skies above, Its glo-ries no tongue may tell;
4. O Zi-on, blest Zi-on, it standeth sure, Its beauties may not wax old;

There standeth a cit-y, we long to be With-in it for-ev-er-more.
Nor sinning, nor sor-row can enter there, For there do they do His will.
'Tis there in the light of the Savior's love, The pu-ri-fied peo-ple dwell.
The walls they are all of the jas-per pure, Its streets of the glitt'ring gold.

CHORUS.

O beautiful home! where the bright ones roam, Where they drink of the stream of life,

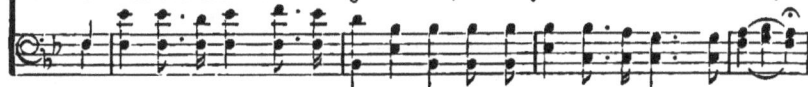

We long to be there, where they know no care, Where there cometh no sound of strife.

No. 160.   ALL MY LIFE LONG.

JOSEPHINE POLLARD.   C. E. POLLOCK. By per.

1. All my life long have my steps been at-tend-ed Sure-ly by
2. All in the dark would I be, and un-cer-tain Whither to
3. He will not wea-ry, O bless-ed as-sur-ance! In-fi-nite

One who re-gard-ed my ways; Ten-der-ly watched o-ver,
go, but for One at my side, Who from the fu-ture re-
love will the fi-nite out-last; But for my heav-en-ly

sweet-ly be-friend-ed, Bless-ings have fol-low'd my nights and my
moves the dim cur-tain Lin-ing the glo-ry to mor-tals de-
Fa-ther's as-sur-ance, In-to the depths of de-spair I were

days; Tears have been quenched in the sun-shine of gladness, Anthems of
nied; No oth-er friend could so pa-tient-ly lead me, No oth-er
cast; This is my star in a mid-night of sor-row, This is my

All My Life Long.

sor - row been turned in - to song: An - gels have guard - ed the
friend prove so faith - ful and strong: With an - gels' food He has
ref - uge, my strength and my song; Earth is to - day, but there's

gate-ways of sad - ness, Sum - mer and win - ter, yea, all my life long.
prom-ised to feed me, Who hath be-friend-ed me all my life long.
heav - en to - mor - row, And Je - sus will guide me all my life long.

No. 161. INTERNATIONAL SUNDAY SCHOOL HYMN.

(Air, "John Brown's Body.")

1 Hail our glorious Leader, mighty Captain of our band!
Listen, comrades, listen to the word of His command;
Lift His banner higher, let it float o'er all the land;
    Still follow where He leads.

CHORUS.—Follow, follow Christ our Leader,
    Loyal hearts, be true to Him forever,
    Naught on earth from Him shall sever;
        He leads to victory.

2 Lo! a mighty army is the Sunday-School to-day;
See its royal colors as it marches on its way:
Jesus goes before us while we watch and fight and pray,
    And follow where He leads.

3 Enemies are 'round us, there are fears and foes within;
Jesus will defend us as we face the hosts of sin;
Trusting in our Captain, we the victory shall win;
    We follow where He leads.

4 Hear the tread of thousands that are falling into line!
Welcome, comrades, welcome, for our Leader is divine;
Forward, at His signal, till the lights of heaven shine;
    Still follow where He leads.

                                    JULIA H. JOHNSTON.

No. 162.　　THE LORD IS RISEN.

MINNIE C. BALLARD.

E. B. SMITH. By per.

1. The Lord, the Lord is ris - en! Ex - ult - ing an-gels sing!
2. No more shall men in an-guish His bleed - ing wounds sur-vey,
3. Bring flow - ers, sweetest flow - ers, His path - way to a - dorn,

He's left the grave's dark pris-on, And death has lost its sting.
No more dis - ci - ples lan-guish, He comes! the Star of day.
And hail the joy - ous hours Of this fair East - er morn.

REFRAIN.

The Lord, the Lord is ris - en! Ex - ult - ing an - gels sing!

He's left the grave's dark prison, And death has lost its sting.
And death has lost, has lost its sting.
And death, and death has lost its sting.

No. 163. BEAUTIFUL STAR OF BETHLEHEM.

(For Christmas.)

MATTIE PEARSON SMITH. J. M. STILLMAN. By per.

1. Beau-ti-ful star of Bethlehem, shine O-ver the hills of Pal-es-tine,
2. Beau-ti-ful star of Bethlehem, shine. Shedding thy beauteous rays di-vine,
3. Beau-ti-ful star of Bethlehem, shine In-to the hearts that faint and pine,
4. Beau-ti-ful star of Bethlehem, shine O-ver this earthly home of mine,

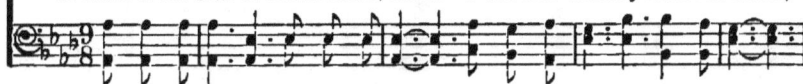

There the Child Jesus slumbereth sweet, And we would bow at His blessed feet.
Light the dark places held in sin's thrall, Bringing thy peace and good-will to all.
Show the Child Jesus, humble, but King, Born to compassion and comfort bring.
How the dear Jesus, dwelling with me, Keepeth me pure and from sinning free.

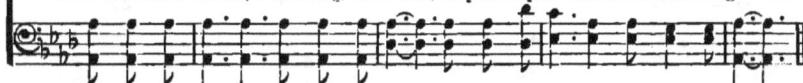

REFRAIN.

Beau-ti-ful star of Beth-le-hem, shine O-ver the hills of Pal-es-tine,
Beau-ti-ful star of Beth-le-hem, shine, Shedding thy beauteous rays di-vine.
Beau-ti-ful star of Beth-le-hem, shine Into the hearts that faint and pine,
Beau-ti-ful star of Beth-le-hem, shine In - to this earthly home of mine,

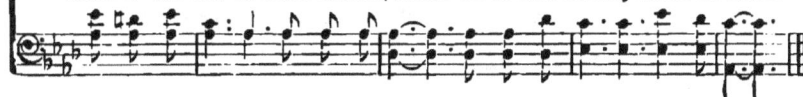

Beau-ti - ful star of Beth-le-hem, shine O-ver the hills of Pal-es-tine.
Beau-ti - ful star of Beth-le-hem, shine, Shedding thy beau-teous rays di-vine.
Beau-ti - ful star of Beth-le-hem, shine Into the hearts that faint and pine.
Beau-ti - ful star of Beth-le-hem, shine In-to this earthly home of mine.

No. 164. BIRTH OF CHRIST THE LORD.

W. A. O.   W. A. Ogden. By per.

1. "Glo - ry to God!" the an - gels are sing - ing, Ti-dings of
2. "Glo - ry to God!" the won-der - ful cho - rus! "Peace and good-
3. "Glo - ry to God!" the mul - ti - tude sing - eth, Glo - ry to

joy to men they bring; Beth-le-hem's plain with mu - sic is
will," the an - gels sing, For un - to you is born in the
God! let men re - ply; Glo - ry to God! the ech - o still

ring - ing, Je - sus to - day is born a King; Not in a
cit - y, Cit - y of Da - vid, Christ a King; Born to re -
ring - eth, Ring-eth a - loud thro' earth and sky; Na-tions shall

pal - ace, but in a man-ger Li-eth the dear Re-deem-er's head,
deem, oh, mighty sal - va - tion! Je-sus, the Christ, oh, yes, 'tis He!
sit no long-er in darkness, Tell the good news o'er earth a - far!

Birth of Christ the Lord.

Gird - ed with glo - ry sag - es be - hold Him, Low where the
Wrapped in the swad-dling garments be - hold Him, This un - to
Seat - ed in glo - ry now be - hold Him, Je - sus the

CHORUS.

beasts of the stall are fed. "Glo-ry to God,"........ the an-gels are
you a sign shall be.
bright and Morn-ing Star. "Glo-ry to God,"

singing, "Peace and good-will"........ to men they bring; Bethlehem's plain........
"Peace and good-will" Bethlehem's plain

with mu-sic is ring-ing, Je-sus to - day.......... is born a King.
Je-sus to-day

No. 165. STAND UP, STAND UP FOR JESUS.

GEO. DUFFIELD.   GEO. WEBB.

FINE.

1. { Stand up, stand up for Je - sus, Ye sol-diers of the cross;
   { Lift high your royal ban - ner, It must not [*Omit.*]   suf-fer loss:
D.C.—*Till ev - 'ry foe is vanquished, And Christ is* [*Omit.*]   *Lord in-deed.*

D C.

From vic - t'ry un - to   vic - t'ry, His   ar - my shall He   lead,

2 Stand up, stand up for Jesus,
  Stand in His strength alone;
  The arm of flesh will fail you,
  Ye dare not trust your own;
  Put on the gospel armor,
  Each piece put on with prayer;
  Where duty calls, or danger,
  Be never wanting there.

3 Stand up, stand up for Jesus
  The strife will not be long;
  This day the noise of battle,
  The next the victor's song.
  To him that overcometh,
  A crown of life shall be;
  He with the King of glory
  Shall reign eternally.

No. 166.   GO FORTH.

(Sing to Tune Above.)

1 Go forth, go forth to battle!
  Tho' strong the foe may be,
  The mighty God of battles
  Is stronger far than he;
  Thy faith shall be thine armor,
  And love shall keep it bright:
  No one can be the victor
  Unless he stand and fight.

2 Go forth, see now God's kingdom
  Besieged by giants grim:
  Smite right and left with vigor,
  And show thy love for Him.

  Be watchful; never sleepeth
  The enemy of souls:
  He would rejoice to gather
  Thy soul among the spoils.

3 Go forth, go forth to battle,
  That may be fierce and strong,
  But measured by God's future,
  At best 'twill not be long:
  Fear not, tho' Satan's legions
  Loud vaunt with boastful words.
  But think with exultation,
  "The battle is the Lord's."

MATTIE PEARSON SMITH.

No. 167.   OH, THEN FOLLOW JESUS.

Mrs. E. C. Ellsworth.   J. Calvin Bushey. By per.

1. Will you from the Sav-ior turn a-way? There is life with-in His word;
2. Will you from the Sav-ior turn a - way, Worshiping at mammon's shrine?
3. Will you from the Sav-ior turn a-way? Near the gate your footsteps press;

Just one step may lead you far a-stray, Nev - er-more to find your Lord.
Lo, your i-dols soon shall turn to clay; How can pleasure then be thine?
Oh, let naught your progress now delay, Soon your soul shall peace possess.

CHORUS.

Oh, then fol-low Je - sus, yielding all, Know no will but His a - lone;

'Tis a childlike spir - it Je-sus loves; Led by love, we are His own.

No. 168. I'LL HAVE NOTHING TO DO WITH RUM.

WM. H. BISHOP.   T. MARTIN TOWNE.

1. I would not own a grog-ger-y, Nor keep a liq-uor store,
2. I would not sell the poisoned dram, To raise the murd'rer's knife,
3. I would not meet the Judgment Day, And God's ap-prov-al crave,
4. I would not vote for li-cense laws, And thus pro-tect the trade;

For all the val-ue of the globe In pre-cious gold-en ore.
To make a mad-dened drunkard seek To take his broth-er's life.
And face the ma-ny thousands there, Who filled the drunkard's grave.
Lest at the judg-ment seat of God, Guilt-y with Him I'm made.

CHORUS.

I'll have noth-ing to do with rum, Mad'ning rum, mad'ning rum,

I'll have noth-ing to do with rum, Rum, rum, mad'ning rum.

TOUCH NOT, TASTE NOT, HANDLE NOT.
No. 169.

Rev. J. B. Atchinson.   W. S. Marshall. By per.

1. Who hath sorrow, who hath woe? They who dare not answer, No!
2. Who hath babblings, who hath strife? He who leads a drunkard's life.
3. Who hath wounds without a cause? He who breaks God's holy laws;
4. Who hath redness in the eyes? Who bring poverty and sighs
5. Touch not, taste not, handle not, Wine will make a dark, dark blot;

They whose feet to sin in-cline; They who tar - ry long at wine.
He who scorns the Lord di-vine, He who goes to seek mixed wine.
He whose lov'd ones weep and pine, While he tar - ries at the wine.
In - to homes al - most di - vine? They who tar - ry at the wine.
Like an ad - der it will sting, And at last to ru - in bring.

Chorus.

They who tar-ry at the wine-cup, They who tarry at the wine-cup,

They who tar-ry at the wine-cup, They have sorrow, they have woe.

No. 170.

1 My country, 'tis of thee,
Sweet land of liberty,
Of thee I sing;
Land where my fathers died,
Land of the Pilgrims' pride,
From every mountain side,
Let freedom ring

2 My native country, thee,
Land of the noble free,
Thy name I love;
I love thy rocks and rills,
Thy woods and templed hills,
My heart with rapture thrills,
Like that above.

3 Let music swell the breeze,
And ring from all the trees
Sweet freedom's song;
Let mortal tongues awake,
Let all that breathe partake,
Let rocks their silence break,
The sound prolong.

4 Our father's God, to Thee,
Author of liberty,
To Thee we sing;
Long may our land be bright,
With freedom's holy light,
Protect us by Thy might,
Great God, our King.
S. F. SMITH

No. 171.

1 Touch not the cup, it is death to thy
soul,
Touch not the cup, touch not the cup;
Many I know who have quaffed from
the bowl,
Touch not the cup, touch it not.
Little they thought that the demon was
there;
Blindly they drank and were caught in
its snare;
Then of that death-dealing bowl, oh,
beware;
Touch not the cup, touch it not.

2 Touch not the cup, oh, drink not a
drop,
Touch not the cup, touch not the cup;
All that thou lovest entreat thee to
stop,
Touch not the cup, touch it not.
Stop for the home that to thee is so
near,
Stop for the home that to thee is so
dear,
Stop, for thy country, the God that you
fear;
Touch not the cup, touch it not.

3 Touch not the cup, when the wine
glistens bright,
Touch not the cup, touch not the cup;
Though like the ruby, it shines in the
light,
Touch not the cup, touch it not.
Fangs of the serpent are hid in the
bowl,
Deeply the poison will enter thy soul,
Soon will it plunge thee beyond thy
control;
Touch not the cup, touch it not.

No. 172.

1 No other love so mighty,
No other love so true:
The depths of mortal trouble
The blessed Jesus knew.

Cho.—No other love so watchful,
Our very thoughts are known:
The Helper's always with us;
We need not bear alone.

2 No loneliness of sorrow,
No bitterness of grief,
Need keep us back from asking
His love for sweet relief.

3 Our days may all be tempest,
Each morning bring us pain;
No other love availeth
To make our losses gain.

4 Not crumbs, but His great riches,
Fall to His children's share,
Tho' poor, unknown, despairing,
Sure of a welcome there.
M. S. SIBLEY.

No. 173.

As Thou hast died for me,
Oh, may my love to Thee,
Pure, warm, and changeless be,
A living fire.

1 What a friend we have in Jesus,
All our sins and griefs to bear!
What a privilege to carry
Everything to God in prayer!
Oh, what peace we often forfeit,
Oh, what needless pain we bear,
All because we do not carry
Everything to God in prayer!

2 Have we trials and temptations?
Is there trouble anywhere?
We should never be discouraged,
Take it to the Lord in prayer.
Can we find a friend so faithful
Who will all our sorrows share?
Jesus knows our every weakness,
Take it to the Lord in prayer.

3 Are we weak and heavy laden,
Cumbered with a load of care?—
Precious Savior, still our refuge,—
Take it to the Lord in prayer.
Do thy friends despise, forsake thee?
Take it to the Lord in prayer:
In His arms He'll take and shield thee,
Thou wilt find a solace there.

3 While life's dark maze I tread,
And griefs around me spread,
Be Thou my Guide;
Bid darkness turn to day,
Wipe sorrow's tears away,
Nor let me ever stray
From Thee aside.

4 When ends life's transient dream,
When death's cold, sullen stream
Shall o'er me roll;
Blest Savior, then, in love,
Fear and distrust remove;
Oh, bear me safe above,
A ransomed soul.

Rev. RAY PALMER.

No. 175.

1 Defend me from my foes, O Lord,
Defend me from my foes;
He, who, unharmed, the desert trod,
The desert trial knows.
When worldly wants by Satan told,
Would make me doubt Thy power,
Through need of bread, or strength,
or gold,
Defend me in that hour.

2 Keep me from earthly pride, O Lord,
Keep me from earthly pride,
For oft the tempter shows abroad
False glories far and wide.
Oh, be the kingdom that I seek,
My glory and my grace;
The kingdom of the poor and meek,
The smiling of Thy face.

Rev. W. WYE SMITH.

No. 174.

1 My faith looks up to Thee,
Thou Lamb of Calvary,
Savior divine:
Now hear me while I pray,
Take all my guilt away,
Oh, let me from this day
Be wholly Thine.

2 May Thy rich grace impart
Strength to my fainting heart,
My zeal inspire;

No. 176. HOME, SWEET HOME.

1 'Mid scenes of confusion and creature complaints,
How sweet to the soul is communion with saints;
To find at the banquet of mercy there's room,
And feel in the presence of Jesus at home!

REFRAIN.—Home, home, sweet, sweet home!
Prepare me, dear Savior, for glory, my home.

2 Sweet bonds that unite all the children of peace!
And thrice precious Jesus, whose love cannot cease!
Though oft from Thy presence in sadness I roam,
I long to behold Thee in glory, at home.

3 Whate'er Thou deniest, oh, give me Thy grace,
The Spirit's sure witness, and smiles of Thy face;
Endue me with patience to wait at Thy throne,
And find, even now, a sweet foretaste of home.

4 I long, dearest Lord, in Thy beauties to shine;
No more as an exile in sorrow to pine:
And in Thy dear image arise from the tomb,
With glorified millions to praise Thee at home.

Rev. DAVID DENHAM

No. 177. PORTUGUESE HYMN.

1 How firm a foundation ye saints of the Lord,
Is laid for your faith in His excellent Word!
What more can He say than to you He hath said,
You who unto Jesus for refuge have fled?

2 "Fear not, I am with thee, oh, be not dismayed,
For I am thy God, and will still give thee aid;
I'll strengthen thee, help thee, and cause thee to stand,
Upheld by My righteous, omnipotent hand.

3 "When through the deep waters I call thee to go,
The rivers of woe shall not thee overflow;
For I will be with thee thy troubles to bless,
And sanctify to thee thy deepest distress.

4 "When through fiery trials thy pathway shall lie,
My grace all-sufficient shall be thy supply;
The flame shall not hurt thee: I only design
Thy dross to consume, and thy gold to refine.

5 "The soul that on Jesus hath leaned for repose
I will not, I will not desert to His foes;
That soul, though all hell should endeavor to shake,
I'll never, no, never, no. never forsake."

GEORGE KEITH.

No. 178.

1 The great Physician now is near,
The sympathizing Jesus:
He speaks the drooping heart to cheer,
Oh, hear the voice of Jesus.

CHO.—Sweetest note in seraph song,
Sweetest name on mortal tongue,
Sweetest carol ever sung,
Jesus, blessed Jesus.

2 Your many sins are all forgiven,
Oh, hear the voice of Jesus;
Go on your way in peace to heaven,
And wear a crown with Jesus.

3 His name dispels my doubt and fear,
No other name but Jesus;
Oh, how my soul delights to hear
The precious name of Jesus.

4 And when to that bright world above,
We rise to see our Jesus;
We'll sing around the throne of love
His name, the name of Jesus.

Rev. WILLIAM HUNTER.

No. 179.

1 Faithful in little things.
Lord, may we be,
Joyfully all the way
Working for Thee.
We our account must give,
Help us for Thee to live;
Knowing that everything,
Thou, Lord, dost see.

2 What Thou hast given us
Gladly we use;
Oh, may we never, Lord,
Thy gift abuse.
Great though it be, or small,
Thou rulest over all:
Wisdom to use it, Thou
Wilt not refuse.

3 Talents, if never used,
Surely will rust;
Hid from the light away,
Moulder to dust.
Slighting what Thou hast sent,
Losing what Thou hast lent,
Have we at length betrayed
Thy heavenly trust.

4 So may we labor on,
Joyful alway,
Seeking to know Thy will,
Lest we may stray.
Much did Thy love bestow,
Deeply our hearts will glow,
Waiting Thy word, "Well done,"
That gladsome day.   M. W. S.

No. 180.

1 Sweet hour of prayer! sweet hour of
     prayer!
That calls me from a world of care,
And bids me at my Father's throne
Make all my wants and wishes known:
In seasons of distress and grief,
My soul has often found relief:
||:And oft escaped the tempter's snare,
By thy return, sweet hour of prayer!:||

2 Sweet hour of prayer! sweet hour of
     prayer!
Thy wings shall my petition bear
To Him whose truth and faithfulness
Engage the waiting soul to bless.
And since He bids me seek His face,
Believe His word, and trust His grace,
|:I'll cast on Him my every care,
And wait for thee, sweet hour of
     prayer!:||

3 Sweet hour of prayer! sweet hour of
     prayer!
May I thy consolation share,
Till, from Mount Pisgah's lofty height,
I view my home and take my flight:
This robe of flesh I'll drop, and rise
To seize the everlasting prize.
||:And shout, while passing through
     the air,
Farewell, farewell, sweet hour of
     prayer!:||
Rev. W. W. WALFORD.

INDEX.

TOPICAL INDEX.